The Gluten-Free Casein-Free Soy-Free Cookbook

By

Jennifer Wood

The Gluten-Free Casein-Free Soy-Free Cookbook

Table of Contents

PREFACE by Jennifer Wood   p. 6

PRODUCTS LIST   p. 7-10

BEVERAGES
    HOMEMADE COCONUT MILK   p. 12
    HOMEMADE ALMOND MILK   p. 13
    PEPPERMINT PATTY ICED CAPPUCINO   p. 14

BREAKFAST
    POP TARTS   p. 16
    WAFFLES   p. 17
    CREPES   p. 18
    GRANOLA   p. 19
    CROCK POT CEREAL   p. 20
    HOMEMADE BREAKFAST CEREAL   p. 21
    EASY EGGS   p. 22
    HOT CEREAL   p. 23
    BUCKWHEAT APPLE PANCAKES   p. 24
    BLUEBERRY PANCAKES   p. 25
    FLUFFY PANCAKES   p. 26
    JOHNNY CAKES   p. 27
    APPLESAUCE SANDWICHES   p. 28
    MOCK MAPLE SYRUP   p. 29
    BAKED OATMEAL   p. 30

BREADS
    GLUTEN-FREE FLOUR BLEND   p. 32
    PIZZA CRUST   p. 33
    ZUCCHINI BREAD   p. 34
    BANANA BREAD   p. 35
    PUMPKIN BREAD   p. 36

NO YEAST BREAD   p. 37
IRISH SODA BREAD   p. 38
POPOVERS   p. 39
FLATBREAD   p. 40
PIZZA CRUST #2   p. 41
GRAIN FREE TORTILLAS   p. 42
ONE MINUTE FLATBREAD   p. 43

SNACKS
BLACK BEAN AND CORN SALSA   p. 45
PEPITAS   p. 46
ANTS ON A LOG   p. 47
COCONUT YOGURT   p. 48
ALMOND YOGURT   p. 49
YOGURT RECIPE #3   P. 50
SWEET CRACKERS   p. 51
HERB CRACKERS   p. 52
MAPLE CORN   p. 53
GLAZED NUTS   p. 54
FRUIT GELATIN   p. 55
TROPICAL POPS   p. 56
FUDGE POPS   p. 57
NACHOS   p. 58
MINI PIZZAS   p. 59

SOUPS, SALADS AND SIDE DISHES
CONDENSED CREAM OF CELERY SOUP   p. 61
CONDENSED CREAM OF CHICKEN SOUP   p. 62
CARROT SALAD   p. 63
QUINOA TABOULEH   p. 64
BERRY TOSSED SALAD   p. 65
QUINOA PILAF   p. 66
ZUCCHINI ROUNDS   p. 67
SWEET POTATO FRIES   p. 68
SPEEDY SPUDS   p. 69
MASHED POTATO CAKES   p. 70
SPICED CARROT STRIPS   p. 71
CANDIED SWEET POTATOES   p. 72
MASHED FAUX-TATOES   p. 73

MAIN DISHES
- SHAKE-N-BAKE CHICKEN   p. 75
- MAKEOVER MEAT LOAF   p. 76
- TUNA CHOWDER   p. 77
- CREAMY CHICKEN AND RICE SOUP   p. 78
- BAKED ZITI   p. 79
- SLOW COOKER CURRIED CHICKEN   p. 80
- CHICKEN-A-LA-KING   p. 81
- STUFFED PEPPERS   p. 82
- SHEPHERD'S PIE   p. 83
- CRUSTLESS QUICHE   p. 84
- TATER TOT CASSEROLE   p. 85
- SALMONETTES   p. 86
- CREAMY CHICKEN OVER RICE   p 87
- CHICKEN AND BISCUITS   p. 88
- HEARTY CHICKEN CASSEROLE   p. 89
- HONEY-MUSTARD CHICKEN   p. 90
- MEXICAN CHICKEN   p. 91
- BBQ GRILLED CHICKEN   p. 92
- DEVILED CHICKEN   p. 93
- POUR PIZZA   p. 94
- ITALIAN BEEF   p. 95
- SALISBURY STEAK   p. 96
- CALZONES   p. 97
- TASTES LIKE PORT-A-PIT CHICKEN   p. 98
- CAJUN BURGERS   p. 99
- CHICKEN ITALIANO   p. 100
- SOUTHWESTERN GOULASH   p. 101
- TUNA BURGERS   p. 102
- BAKED CHICKEN NUGGETS   p. 103
- QUINOA PIZZA BITES   p. 104
- MINI CHICKEN POT PIES   p. 105
- POP-OVER PIZZA   p. 106
- SWEET BARBECUE CHICKEN   p. 107
- MOM'S CHICKEN AND RICE   p. 108

DESSERTS
- FRUIT ICE CREAM   p. 110
- MINT CHIP ICE CREAM   p. 111
- NO ROLL PIE CRUST #1   p. 112
- FRUIT PIE   p. 113
- NO ROLL PIE CRUST #2   p. 114
- NO CRUST PUMPKIN PIE   p. 115
- PEACH COBBLER   p. 116
- CHOCOLATE PEANUT BUTTER PIE   p. 117
- BLUEBERRY COFFEE CAKE   p. 118
- BROWNIES   p. 119
- STRAWBERRY PUFF   p. 120
- CUSTARD PIE   p. 121
- FRUIT CRISP   p. 122
- BAKED APPLES   p. 123
- RICE KRISPIE TREATS   p. 124
- APPLESAUCE CAKE   p. 125
- KOPYKAT KIT KAT BARS   p. 126
- CHOCOLATE BARS   p. 127
- PUMPKIN CUSTARD   p. 128
- CHOCOLATE BALLS   P. 129
- APPLE STRUESEL PIE   p. 130
- CHOCOLATE NO BAKE BARS   p. 131
- CARROT CAKE   p. 132
- CHOCOLATE CHIP COOKIES   p. 133
- CANDY CANE KISSES   p. 134

SPECIAL THANKS AND ACKNOWLEGEMENTS p. 135

ABOUT THE AUTHOR   p. 136

Preface

By Jennifer Wood

I wrote this cookbook to help others with food allergies/food sensitivities to be able to make recipes that both tasted good and were comfort foods. My daughter and I both have similar food allergies and food sensitivities. I am actually more sensitive than she is, in the fact that she can tolerate some dairy, and I am not able to tolerate any at all. She can also have any gluten free grain without it bothering her. I am very sensitive to rice, which is unfortunately in almost every gluten free, pre-packaged food. I feel better when I only eat the "pseudo" grains (like quinoa, amaranth, buckwheat, or nut flours). I do want to point out that I try to make most of my recipes lower in sugar, and free from heavily refined sugars. Most of the recipes that would normally call for sugar, I replaced with stevia, xylitol, honey, or coconut sugar. If sugar is not a concern, feel free to replace the sugar substitutes with regular sugar. Also, if you are just doing a gluten-free diet, you can replace the non-dairy items with dairy.

Products List

Most of the products I use are bought online, or at our local co-op. I buy organic grains in their whole grain form in bulk in twenty-five pound bags, and then grind them myself. Certain grains I am not able to buy in bulk, and I get those online. I am very careful to avoid products that contain Genetically Modified Organisms (GMO's). I get most of my products at places like Vitacost (www.vitacost.com) or Swanson Vitamins (www.swansonvitamins.com). The NOW brand products are at Swanson, but not at Vitacost.

All of the items listed below can be found at either Vitacost or Swanson, unless specified. The brands I list are GFCFSF, along with GMO free. I use these items on a regular basis:

1. Tapioca flour – Bob's Red Mill

2. Stevia – I use NOW brand Stevia Glycerite liquid. It doesn't have alcohol, and doesn't have an aftertaste. Kal brand pure stevia powder is also good.

3. Nutiva Extra Virgin coconut oil –has a mild flavor, and is good priced.

4. Xylitol – The Ultimate Sweetener by Ultimate Life is good, and is made from birch trees instead of corn. XyloSweet brand is also good. It does come from a corn source, but is non-GMO.

5. Coconut Sugar – Coconut Secret and Madhava are both good brands.

6. Xanthan gum –Bob's Red Mill

7. Potato Starch – Bob's Red Mill or the Ener-G brand. .

8. Potato Flour – Both Bob's Red Mill and the Ener-G brand

9. Cocoa Powder – NOW brand organic cocoa powder or the Swanson brand is good

10. Carob Powder – NOW brand or Bob's Red Mill

11. Garbanzo/Chickpea Flour – Bob's Red Mill

12. Honey – Buying locally is best (especially if it is unheated). YS Bee Farm offers both raw honey and regular clove.

13. Shredded Coconut – Bob's Red Mill. Tropical Traditions has shredded coconut in bulk (www.tropicaltraditions.com).

14. Pasta – Tinkyada Brown Rice pasta is the best. Their pasta tastes like regular white flour pasta. It comes in elbows, spirals, spaghetti, lasagna, penne and several other varieties. Orgran brand buckwheat pasta is also good.

15. Ghee – Purity Farms Ghee is labeled as casein-free. They have a large size (13 ounces) available.

16. Baking Powder – Bob's Red Mill offers a 16 ounce bag. It is labeled as gluten-free and aluminum free.

17. Baking Soda – Bob's Red Mill offers this also in a 16 ounce bag, and it is labeled gluten-free and aluminum free.

18. Sea Salt – Redmond Sea Salt is excellent, and comes in a large 26 ounce bag. This is the only salt I use.

19. Egg Replacer – Ener-G brand is gluten-free. Both websites offer this.

20. Almond Flour – I have used NOW brand, but also buy in bulk online wherever is cheapest. Almond flour can also be made with a food processor.

21. Chia Seeds – I have only tried Nutiva, but there are several other brands listed on both websites.

22. Vanilla – I like the Simply Organic Vanilla Extract. Frontier brand also makes a good one.

23. Crispy Rice Cereal – Nature's Path and Barbara's Bakery Brown Rice Crisps.

24. Arrowroot Powder – Bob's Red Mill.

25. Agar Agar Powder – NOW brand

There are many other grains available from these websites, if you are not able to find a good source in bulk.

Other items I use regularly, that I am not able to buy online:

1. Cheese – Daiya brand is the only cheese I have been able to find that tastes the closest to real cheese, and melts like cheese. It is casein and lactose free. It is also free of soy, gluten, eggs, peanuts and tree nuts. Our grocery store now carries it! If your local grocery, health food store or co-op doesn't sell it, ask them to!

2. Lunchmeat – Hormel has natural deli meat that is free of gluten, nitrates and nitrites. It is available in ham, turkey and roast beef.

3. Hot Dogs – Shelton's has turkey and chicken dogs that are free of nitrates, and are GFCFSF. Oscar Meyer also has nitrate-free hot dogs.

4. Coconut Milk – If I am not able to make my own, the brand I like to use is So Delicious. If that isn't available in your area, you can use the Thai Kitchen brand in the cans. Natural Value brand is additive free, which is a help for those with sensitivities to additives.

5. Almond Milk – If I am not able to make my own, I use Almond Breeze by Blue Diamond or the Silk brand.

***A note on grains:
Most grains are cheapest to buy in bulk, and in their whole grain form. Many grains, like quinoa, can be hard to find in flour form. Whole grains can be ground in almost any blender, if done in quantities of 1-2 cups. If you are on a budget, grinding your own grain is usually the most cost effective way to eat gluten-free grains.

Beverages

Homemade Coconut Milk

I love the convenience of carton and canned coconut milk, but do not love the additives like carrageenan and guar gum. Both additives are notorious for causing digestive distress. With homemade milk, you end up with two products instead of just one.

¾ cup shredded coconut
4 cups hot water (not boiling)

Place the shredded coconut and hot water in a blender, and allow the water to cool for 30 minutes. Blend well, then strain through a very fine mesh strainer to remove pulp **. Refrigerate.

For thick milk (like the kind you buy in the can):
1 cup shredded coconut
2 cups hot water

Repeat the steps as instructed above.

**Do not throw your coconut pulp away!! Save it in glass jars, and place in the freezer until you have a large amount of pulp. Thaw the pulp out, and spread onto a cookie sheet. Bake at a very low temperature (as low as your oven can go) until the coconut pulp is dry. You can also use a dehydrator to dry the pulp, if you have one. Once dry, allow the dried pulp to cool. Pulverize in a food processor or blender to a fine powder. You now have coconut flour that can be used in other baking recipes!

Homemade Almond Milk

Almond milk is another store-bought product that contains additives like carrageenan and guar gum.

For thinner milk:
½ cup almonds (preferably soaked for 6-8 hours in water)
4 cups water

Blend in a blender on high until blended well. Strain through very fine mesh strainer **. Refrigerate.

For thicker milk:
1 cup almonds
4 cups water

Follow same steps as above.

*Do not throw your almond pulp away!! Save it in glass jars, and place in the freezer until you have a large amount of pulp. Thaw the pulp out, and spread onto a cookie sheet. Bake at a very low temperature (as low as your oven can go) until the almond pulp is dry. Once dry, allow the dried pulp to cool. Pulverize in a food processor or blender to a fine powder. You now have almond flour that can be used in other baking recipes!

Peppermint Patty Iced Cappucino

1/2 c. coffee (fresh, not instant)
1/2 c. dairy-free milk (I used coconut)
2 t. cocoa powder
1/4-1/2 tsp. liquid stevia (omit and add sweetener of choice if you don't like stevia)
2 T. honey (or more to taste)
1 c. ice
1-2 drops food grade peppermint oil (I used Young Living)

Blend all ingredients in a blender until smooth.

Breakfast Recipes

Pop Tarts

It is hard to imagine healthy pop tarts, but these are. These are healthy enough for breakfasts, snacks or desserts.

1 cup almond flour
1 ½ cups gluten-free flour blend (p. 32)
1 tsp. cinnamon
½ tsp. salt
2 tsp. xanthan gum
3 packets stevia (omit and add preferred sweetener if you do not like stevia)
3 T. honey
½ cup dairy-free milk
2 eggs
¼ cup olive oil
½ cup tapioca flour (or more)
All fruit jam
1 egg (for brushing on top)
Xylitol or sugar (for top)

In a large bowl, combine the almond flour, gluten-free flour blend, cinnamon, salt, xanthan gum, and stevia, mixing well to combine. In a separate bowl, mix the honey, milk, eggs, and olive oil. Add the egg mixture to the dry ingredients. Mix until the dough is wet. Start adding the tapioca flour to the dough until the dough can be kneaded. Roll out dough between 2 large sheets of parchment paper to about 1/8 inch thickness. Cut large rectangles (about 5 inches by 6 inches). Place fruit jam over half of each rectangle. Carefully fold over to make a pouch, and press and seal the edges with a fork. If needed, wet the edges slightly to seal. Beat remaining egg and brush over the tops of the pop tarts. Sprinkle with xylitol or sugar. Bake at 350° for 30-40 minutes until crusts are golden brown.

Waffles

2 c. gluten-free flour (garbanzo, rice, or whatever you prefer)
2 eggs
1 ½ Tbsp. baking powder
2 tsp. xanthan gum
Pinch of salt
2 Tbsp. olive oil
2 Tbsp. honey
½ tsp. liquid stevia (skip the honey and add ½ cup sugar if you don't like stevia)
1 tsp. vanilla extract
2 C. dairy-free milk (coconut, almond, etc.) – more may be needed, depending on which flour is used.

Mix dry ingredients in a bowl. Mix wet ingredients in a separate bowl. Mix all together. Spray waffle iron with nonstick cooking spray, and spread batter onto iron. Make sure you spray the waffle iron before each waffle is put on.

Top with favorite topping. We love ghee with honey, or ghee with maple syrup. Also blended fruit is good on top of this. This makes approximately 4 large waffles.

Crepes

This recipe is very versatile. I have used millet, quinoa, amaranth, flour, buckwheat, garbanzo and rice and almond flour. All were good. If you use millet or almond flour, it does tend to fall apart easier. These cook very well on an electric griddle, but you can also use an oiled non-stick pan.

½ cup gluten-free flour (whatever kind you prefer)
¾ cup dairy-free milk (coconut, almond, etc.)
2 eggs
2 T. olive oil
1 ½ T. sugar or 1/8 tsp. liquid stevia
Pinch of salt
Jam or jelly
Powdered sugar (optional)

Mix batter until there are no lumps. Pour like pancakes onto a greased electric griddle, or into a greased non-stick skillet. Spread batter out with a spatula, so that it is fairly thin. Cook like a pancake, and flip. Place a dollop of jelly or jam in the center, and roll up the crepe. Sprinkle with powdered sugar, if desired.

Granola

Oats are naturally gluten-free, but the problem lies in the fact that they can be contaminated with gluten. Some companies, like Bob's Red Mill, are now selling gluten-free oats that are supposed to be free of any contamination. This is a very easy recipe and a good one if you are able to find a good source for gluten-free oats.

6 cups gluten-free oats
1 cup sunflower seeds
½ cup pumpkin seeds, almonds, cashews or walnuts
½ cup oil (olive oil or melted coconut oil work well)
½ cup honey or maple syrup (you can add more if you want it sweeter)
½ cup water
1 Tbsp. cinnamon
2 tsp. vanilla extract

Mix the oats, sunflower seeds, and the pumpkin seeds (or almonds, cashews or walnuts) together in a large bowl. In a smaller bowl, mix the remaining ingredients together with a wire whisk. Pour the wet mixture over the dry mixture, stirring well so that everything is well moistened.

Divide the mixture between two 9 x 13 inch pans. Bake at 250° for 1½ hours, stirring every ½ hour.

Crock Pot Cereal

Millet is another gluten-free grain that has been controversial because it can be contaminated with gluten. Many gluten-free websites list it as safe, while other websites recommend avoiding it. Arrowhead Mills lists their Hulled Millet as gluten-free, as does Bob's Red Mill. My daughter and I are both able to eat millet without any problems.

1 cup whole millet
4½ cups water
1 tsp. salt
1 tsp. vanilla
1 tsp. cinnamon
½ cup coconut (optional)
½ cup raisins
Sweetener such as honey, maple syrup, or stevia to taste

Place the millet, water, salt, vanilla and cinnamon in a crock pot that has been sprayed with non-stick cooking spray. Cook on low over night. In the morning, add the coconut and raisins, and cook for 5-10 minutes longer. Add your sweetener of choice, and sweeten to taste.

Homemade Breakfast Cereal

Some friends who had lived overseas introduced me to popped rice. I was excited to find that rice was just one of several grains that popped. Of all the grains, amaranth was the most fun to pop. It actually looks like tiny white popcorn, and almost doubles the amount after you are finished popping.

1 tsp. oil (the oil is not necessary, but helps the grains not to pop so high)
1 cup quinoa, rice, amaranth, or millet (whole, not flour)

Put oil into a Dutch oven, and heat on high until droplets of water dance across the pan. Place the grain in the pan, and stir constantly with a wooden spoon. Make sure the grain is always moving. The grain will start to pop in the pan, and some of the grains can pop quite high. Cook until the grain is a golden brown. This doesn't take long! Watch very closely so that it doesn't burn. When finished, pour into a bowl to cool. Add milk and sweetener of choice. Can be eaten warm or cold, and eaten with a spoon.

*This can also be eaten as a snack like popcorn (ghee and salt can be added), eaten with a spoon.

Easy Eggs

4 eggs, beaten
3 slices lunchmeat (Hormel turkey or ham works well), cut up into bite-sized pieces
3 Tbsp. salsa
Dash of salt and pepper
Ghee or coconut oil
Dairy-free cheese (like Daiya), optional

Mix the eggs, lunchmeat, salsa, salt and pepper in a bowl. Scramble the egg mixture in a fry pan with ghee or coconut oil. When the eggs are cooked, add the cheese, if desired, and cover with a lid to melt the cheese.

For our family, this will serve 2 people.

Hot Cereal

Amaranth is a "pseudo" grain. It is actually a seed and not a grain. It is power packed with nutrients. It has more protein than any other gluten-free grain. It also has more calcium, magnesium, iron and fiber than any other gluten-free grain. Amaranth has a strong flavor, but can be masked by adding spices and sweeteners. It is a definitely worth giving amaranth a try, just for its healthy nutrients alone.

4 cups water
1 1/2 cups whole amaranth**
¼ tsp. salt
1 tsp. cinnamon
2 tsp. vanilla extract
3 Tbsp. ghee or casein-free margarine
4 Tbsp. honey, maple syrup, coconut sugar or xylitol
Stevia to taste, optional
Raisins, frozen blueberries or apples

Bring the water to a boil, and add the amaranth. Cover and simmer on low heat for 25-30 minutes, stirring a few times. Cook until the water is cooked off. Add raisins, blueberries or apples during the last 5 minutes of cooking, while there is still water in the pan. When finished cooking, add the salt, cinnamon, vanilla, ghee or margarine, honey (or other sweetener), and optional stevia.

***If amaranth is not available, of not well liked, you can replace it with another gluten-free whole grain such as quinoa or millet.

Buckwheat Apple Pancakes

Despite its name, buckwheat is not part of the wheat family. Buckwheat contains all eight amino acids, and is an excellent source of plant protein. Make sure that your source for buckwheat is not contaminated with wheat. Bob's Red Mill offers buckwheat that is free of contaminations. The buckwheat can be replaced with different flour, if you do not care for buckwheat.

1 cup buckwheat flour
½ cup tapioca flour
3 Tbsp. coconut sugar, xylitol, or regular sugar
1 tsp. xanthan Gum
1 ½ Tbsp. baking powder
Pinch salt
½ tsp. cinnamon
1/8 tsp. nutmeg
2 eggs
½ cup applesauce
1 ½ cups dairy-free milk (or more) - use less if using a different flour besides buckwheat
½ tsp. vanilla extract
1 medium apple, chopped very fine
¼ tsp. liquid stevia (replace with ¼ cup of sugar if you don't like stevia)

Mix ingredients all together. Cook the pancakes on an electric griddle or in an oiled non-stick pan. Top with maple syrup or applesauce.

Blueberry Pancakes

1¼ cups rice or garbanzo flour
1 Tbsp. baking powder
½ tsp. salt
1 tsp. xanthan gum
1¼ cups dairy-free milk (coconut, almond, etc.)
1 Tbsp. vinegar or lemon juice
2. Tbsp. xylitol, coconut sugar, or regular sugar
2 eggs
3 Tbsp. olive oil
Fresh or frozen blueberries

Mix the milk with the vinegar or lemon juice. Set aside. Meanwhile, mix the flour, baking powder, salt, xanthan gum, and sugar. Add eggs and olive oil to the milk mixture, and mix well. Add the milk mixture to the dry ingredients and stir well.

Cook on a hot griddle, adding blueberries to the pancakes when you first put them on the griddle.

Fluffy Pancakes

1 ½ cups garbanzo bean flour
1 T. baking powder
2 eggs
½ - 1 cup dairy-free milk (start with ½ cup and add more if needed to get a thin, pancake batter consistency)
A dash of liquid stevia or 2 Tbsp. sugar

Mix all ingredients together until there are no lumps. Cook on an electric griddle or heavily oiled fry pan.

Johnny Cakes

Johnny Cakes were America's first pancake, made by pioneers and homesteaders. We first made these for a homeschooling lesson we did on pioneers. They are really good, and very easy to make. They do not taste like traditional pancakes, but taste more like grits that have been cooked into a pancake.

1 cup yellow or white cornmeal*
2 Tbsp. xylitol or sugar
½ tsp. salt
1 cup boiling water

Grease a non-stick griddle or non-stick fry pan with oil, ghee or casein free margarine. The Johnny Cakes have a tendency to stick, so make sure you grease the griddle or fry pan. In a bowl, mix the cornmeal, sugar, and salt together. Add the boiling water, stirring constantly until smooth. Batter will be very runny.

Drop onto the griddle or fry pan, making small pancakes. Cook just like pancakes, on medium heat until browned. Serve with maple syrup or honey.

*I have also had success making these with millet flour. If corn is a problem, millet is another option in this recipe.

Applesauce Sandwiches

This recipe is fun for kids and adults alike. It is made like grilled cheese, but with applesauce. They are great for breakfast, or for a snack.

1 cup applesauce
8 slices gluten free bread
4 Tbsp. ghee or casein-free margarine, softened
1 ½ Tbsp. xylitol, coconut sugar, or regular sugar
¼ tsp. ground cinnamon

Evenly spread the applesauce on 4 slices of bread, and top with remaining bread. Spread the ghee or margarine on outsides of the sandwiches. Toast on a hot griddle or fry pan for 3-4 minutes on each side, or until golden brown.

Combine sugar and cinnamon; sprinkle over hot sandwiches. Serve immediately.

Mock Maple Syrup

Maple syrup is a natural food, but for those of us who are sensitive to sugar (even in natural form), it is too sweet. This is a nice alternative, and tastes good on pancakes.

2 c. water, divided
4 packets stevia (I used the NOW brand)
1/2 c. xylitol
½-1 tsp. maple flavoring (I used Frontier brand)
1 1/2 T. arrowroot powder

In a saucepan, add 1 1/2 cups water, the stevia and xylitol. Bring to a boil. Mix arrowroot with the remaining 1/2 cup water, and add to pan. Bring to boil again and boil for 1 minute, stirring constantly. Remove from heat and allow the syrup to cool slightly. Add the maple flavoring. Serve warm on pancakes or waffles. Store any leftovers in a jar in the fridge. Always warm up syrup before serving.

Baked Oatmeal

¼ c. melted coconut oil
¼ c. melted ghee
2 eggs
½ c. maple syrup (or ¼ c. maple syrup plus ½ tsp. stevia for lower sugar)
1 ¼ c. dairy-free milk (add ¼ c. more if using stevia)
3 c. rolled oats
2 tsp. baking powder
1 tsp. salt
Blueberries, raisins, fruit or nuts (optional)

Preheat oven to 350°. Whisk together the coconut oil, ghee, eggs, syrup, stevia (if using) and milk until well blended. In a separate bowl, mix together the oats, baking powder and salt. Pour the wet ingredients over the dry ones and mix.

Place into a greased pan (I used an 8 x 11 inch pan). Cover and bake for 20-25 minutes. Check to see if the oatmeal is cooked all the way through. If not, cover and bake for another 10-15 minutes. Serve with fruit or nuts if desired.

Bread Recipes

Gluten-Free Flour Blend

This recipe is great for so many recipes. I use it on a regular basis. If you rotate grains, you can substitute a different gluten-free flour like buckwheat, quinoa, millet, sorghum or garbanzo in place of the rice.

3 cups rice flour
1 cup potato starch (not potato flour!)
1/2 cup tapioca starch/flour

Mix well, and store in an airtight container in the refrigerator.

<u>Pizza Crust</u>

1 c. gluten-free flour (whatever kind you prefer)
½ cup tapioca flour
1 Tbsp. ground flax seeds
½ tsp. sugar
¼ tsp. baking soda
½ tsp. salt
½ tsp. garlic powder
¼ tsp. onion powder
½ tsp. oregano
2 eggs
Dairy-free milk

Mix dry ingredients together until blended. In a separate bowl, combine the eggs and 1 tablespoon of milk, and mix well. Add to dry ingredients and stir well, adding more milk a tablespoon at a time until the mixture is soft enough to spread with a knife or spatula. If it is too sticky to spread, add a bit more milk. Spread into a well-greased pizza pan out to the edges of the pan with a spatula. Bake at 350° for 10-12 minutes. Add pizza sauce and toppings, and bake pizza as usual.

This recipe makes a thin crust pizza.

Zucchini Bread

1 ½ cups gluten-free flour blend (p. 32)
1 tsp. ground cinnamon
½ tsp. baking soda
¼ tsp. salt
1 tsp. baking powder
1 tsp. xanthan gum
¼ tsp. ground nutmeg
1 cup sugar (for lower sugar, use ½ cup honey and ½ tsp. liquid stevia)
1 cup finely shredded unpeeled zucchini
¼ cup olive oil
2 eggs
1 tsp. vanilla extract

Combine the flour, cinnamon, baking soda, salt, baking powder, xanthan gum and nutmeg in a mixing bowl. In a separate bowl, combine sugar (or honey/stevia mixture), zucchini, oil, eggs, and vanilla. Mix well. Add the flour mixture, and stir until just combined. Pour batter into a greased 8 x 4 x 2 inch loaf pan. Bake at 350° for 40-45 minutes, or until a toothpick inserted near center comes out clean.

Banana Bread

1 ¾ cups gluten-free flour blend (p. 32)
2/3 cup sugar (or 1/3 cup xylitol or honey and ½ tsp. liquid stevia)
1 t. baking powder
½ tsp. baking soda
¼ tsp. salt
1 tsp. xanthan gum
1 cup mashed bananas
1/3 cup olive oil
2 Tbsp. dairy-free milk (or more if needed)
2 eggs
1 tsp. vanilla extract

In a large mixing bowl, combine 1 cup of the flour, along with the sugar or xylitol, baking powder, baking soda, salt and xanthan gum. Add the bananas, oil and milk. Beat with an electric mixer on low until blended, then on high for 2 minutes. Add the stevia (if using) eggs, vanilla and remaining flour, and beat until blended. If batter is too thick, add more milk.

Pour batter into a greased 8 x 4 x 2 inch loaf pan. Bake at 350° for 50-60 minutes, or until a toothpick inserted near center comes out clean. Cool for 10 minutes on wire rack before removing from pan.

Pumpkin Bread

2 cups gluten-free flour blend (p. 32)
1 cup packed brown sugar (or ½ cup coconut sugar and ½ tsp. liquid stevia)
1 Tbsp. baking powder
1 tsp. ground cinnamon
¼ tsp. salt
¼ tsp. baking soda
2 tsp. xanthan gum
¼ tsp. ground nutmeg
1/8 tsp. ground ginger
1/8 tsp. ground cloves
1 cup canned pumpkin
½ cup dairy-free milk (coconut, almond, etc.), or more if needed
2 eggs
¼ cup coconut oil
1 tsp. vanilla extract

In a large bowl, combine 1 cup of flour, the brown sugar (or coconut sugar), baking powder, cinnamon, salt, baking soda, xanthan gum, nutmeg, ginger, and cloves. Add pumpkin, stevia (if using in the recipe), milk, eggs, coconut oil and vanilla. Beat with an electric mixer on low until blended, then on high for 2 minutes. Add remaining flour and beat well.
Pour batter into a greased 9 x 5 x 3 inch loaf pan. Bake at 350° for 60-65 minutes or until a toothpick, inserted near the center, comes out clean.

No Yeast Bread

I have tried this recipe with many different gluten-free flours, and the best tasting are rice flour and garbanzo flour. Experiment with other grains to see which ones you prefer. This bread can be pre-sliced and then frozen.

2 cups rice flour, garbanzo flour, or gluten-free flour blend (p. 32)
3 Tbsp. sugar or xylitol
2 tsp. baking powder
½ tsp. baking soda
2 tsp. xanthan gum
2 large eggs
1 cup dairy-free milk, with 1 Tbsp. vinegar or lemon juice (to make buttermilk)
2 Tbsp. olive oil

Mix flour, sugar, baking powder, baking soda, and xanthan gum in a large bowl. In a smaller bowl, combine the eggs, milk and oil. Stir the wet ingredients into the dry ingredients, and mix until just moistened. Do not over mix.

Spread the batter into a greased 8 x 4 x 2 inch loaf pan, and bake at 350° for 45 minutes. Remove from the pan, and cool on a wire rack.

Irish Soda Bread

I modified this recipe from an old family favorite. This recipe is great for St. Patrick's Day, for breakfast, or for an addition to any meal.

2 ½ cups gluten-free flour blend (p. 32)
¼ cup brown sugar (or coconut sugar or xylitol)
1 tsp. baking powder
1 tsp. baking soda
1 tsp. salt
1 tsp. xanthan gum
3 Tbsp. ghee or casein-free margarine
1 cup dairy-free milk mixed with 1 Tbsp. lemon juice or vinegar (to make buttermilk)
1 egg
1/2 cup raisins
1 Tbsp. ghee or casein free margarine, melted

In a bowl, combine flour, brown sugar, baking powder, baking soda, salt and xanthan gum. Cut in ghee or margarine until crumbly. Combine egg and buttermilk; stir into the flour mixture until just moistened. Fold in raisins.

Knead on tapioca or rice floured surface for about a minute. Shape into a round loaf, and place on a greased baking sheet. Cut a ¼ inch deep cross on top of the loaf. Bake at 350° for 40-45 minutes or until toothpick inserted near the center comes out clean. Remove from the oven and brush the melted ghee or margarine over the bread. Cool on a wire rack for 10 minutes.

Popovers

These are very versatile. They can be eaten plain, or topped with nut butter or jam. They can also be stuffed with egg salad, chicken salad or tuna salad, or with lunchmeat. To reheat them, just pop them into a toaster oven. I usually double the recipe because we eat them up so quickly!

1 cup tapioca starch/flour (other gluten-free flours can be used instead)
3 eggs
½ tsp. salt
1 tsp. baking powder
½ tsp. xanthan gum
1 cup dairy-free milk
1 Tbsp. oil

Preheat oven to 425°. Mix ingredients together in a bowl until there are no lumps. Pour into greased muffin tins, about halfway full.

Bake for 20 minutes. Reduce the heat to 350°, and bake for another 20-25 minutes. This recipe makes 12 popovers.

Flatbread

When I first concocted this recipe, I used quinoa flour, which is normally a strong flavored grain. The flavor was masked well by the herbs. Experiment with different gluten free flours to see which one you like best. This bread makes great sandwiches.

1½ cups gluten-free flour (rice, garbanzo, or whatever flour you prefer)
¾ cup tapioca flour
1/3 cup ground flax seeds
½ tsp. baking soda
1 tsp. salt
1½ tsp. oregano
½ tsp. garlic powder
1 tsp. basil
½ tsp. xanthan gum
½ cup dairy-free milk (more if needed)
3 eggs
1 tsp. honey

Preheat oven to 350°. In a large bowl, combine dry ingredients. Mix well until blended together. In a small bowl, whisk together the milk, eggs and honey until very well mixed, whisking for about 1 minute.

Pour egg mixture into flour mixture and stir well, adding more milk if dough is too thick. Dough needs to be soft enough to spread into a pan with a spatula or knife. Line a cookie sheet with parchment paper. Spread the dough out evenly to the edges of the pan, making sure it is even. Bake for 8-10 minutes, or until toothpick inserted near center comes out clean. Do not over bake, or it will be too dry. Cool and cut into desired sizes.

*For sweet bread, add 1 tablespoon cinnamon, ½ tsp. liquid stevia and a pinch of salt in place of the 1 tsp. salt, garlic powder, oregano, and basil.

Pizza Crust #2

Flatbread recipe from previous page
Olive oil
Garlic
Salt
Spices (such as oregano, basil, Italian Seasoning)

Preheat oven to 350°. Prepare flatbread according to the recipe above. Place the dough on a pizza pan**.Spread the dough out to the edges of the pan. Make a crust all around the edges. Brush the entire crust with olive oil, and sprinkle garlic, salt, and spices. Bake for 12-15 minutes. Take crust out of oven and top with sauce and toppings of choice. Place back in oven and bake until pizza is cooked.

**I have made this recipe without using the parchment paper. It did stick quite a bit. If you do not use parchment paper, make sure to oil your pan well before the dough is put in the pan.

Grain Free Tortillas

These are a bit time consuming, but very easy because there is no rolling required.

1 cup arrowroot powder (or cornstarch if you don't have arrowroot)
1 cup tapioca starch
2 tsp. salt
2 Tbsp. Italian Seasoning (sounds like a lot, but gives it amazing flavor)
1 tsp. garlic powder
1 tsp. onion powder
1½ cups dairy-free milk
4 eggs

Mix all ingredients together in a bowl, making sure it is free of lumps. You can make these in a non-stick skillet, or you can do them on an electric skillet. I used an electric skillet because I could make more than one at once. Pour a small pancake size amount onto your skillet. If using an electric skillet, spread the batter out with a spatula, making a large crepe. If using a regular skillet, as you pour the batter, pick up the skillet and move it so that the batter spreads around the pan. Cook like a pancake, and flip when ready. Cool on a wire rack so that they don't stick together.

This recipe makes about 14 large wraps. I like to freeze them in layers between parchment paper, and pull them out when I need them. To reheat them, place them in a toaster oven or regular oven on the rack and heat until warm. Do not heat them too long or they will get crisp. The recipe can be cut in half or doubled.

***Note: if you make these in a non-stick skillet, do not
use a lot of oil, as it could make the tortillas gummy. Non-stick cooking spray would probably work fine, but test first to make sure the spray doesn't make the tortillas gummy.

One Minute Flatbread

This is a very easy recipe that can be used for bread, pizza crust, or for hamburger buns. This recipe is for one person, but can be doubled, tripled, etc.

¼ cup gluten-free flour (I use garbanzo)
½ tsp. baking powder
1 tsp. olive oil
1 egg
Dash salt
½-1 Tbsp. dairy-free milk
Seasonings*

In a bowl, mix ingredients until well blended. Start with ½ Tablespoon of milk, and add more if needed if batter is too thick. Spread the batter thinly onto a parchment lined plate in shape of choice and microwave for 1 minute. The bread can also be placed on a parchment lined pan and baked in the oven at 350° for 10-12 minutes. For hamburger buns, spray a ramekin dish with nonstick cooking spray and pour the mixed batter into the dish. Bake at 350° for 10-15 minutes, until it is cooked through.

*For herb bread, add garlic, salt, and Italian seasoning, or whatever herbs and spices you prefer. For sweet bread, add cinnamon and sweetener of your choice (I used stevia).

Snacks

Black Bean and Corn Salsa

1 can (15 ounces) black beans, rinsed
1 can (16 ounces) corn, drained
½ cup slices olives
½ cup chopped onions
1½ cups chopped tomatoes
¼ cup chopped fresh cilantro
6 Tbsp. lime juice
1½ tsp. cumin
½ tsp. salt

In a bowl, combine the beans, corn, olives, onions, tomatoes and cilantro. In a small bowl, Mix the lime juice, cumin and salt. Pour over the bean mixture and stir well. Serve with chips, or in a tortilla.

**The salsa can be eaten right away, or can be chilled for a few hours to allow the flavors to mingle.

Pepitas

Pepitas are shelled pumpkin seeds that are roasted in the oven with seasonings. These are great as a snack or on salads. I'm actually including two different ways to do these. If you have a dehydrator, you can dry the pepitas at a lower temperature for a longer length of time. This is more nutritious, and the seeds are easier to digest. If you have a dehydrator with a thermostat, you can dry the seeds at 115° or lower, and the seeds will still be considered raw.

Oven roasted:
2 cups raw pumpkin seeds, hulled
1/2 Tbsp. olive oil
½-1 salt, or to taste
½ tsp. garlic powder

Preheat oven to 300°. Mix ingredients together in a bowl until well combined. Spread the pumpkin seeds on a cookie sheet so that they are not overlapping. Bake for 20-30 minutes, or until lightly browned, stirring once or twice.

Dehydrator recipe:
Soak the pumpkin seeds in water and 1 tsp. salt for 8-10 hours. Drain, but don't rinse the seeds. Add salt and garlic to taste (do not add the oil), then place on dehydrator trays, making sure not to overlap the seeds. Dehydrate until seeds are the desired crispiness.

Ants On A Log

This is a fun snack for kids and adults! The honey gives it a hint of sweetness that compliments the raisins.

5 stalks of celery
½ cup peanut butter, almond butter, cashew butter, or sunflower butter
1-2 Tbsp. honey
¼ cup raisins

Mix the nut butter and honey together. Spread on the stalks of celery. Top with raisins.

Coconut Yogurt

1 quart coconut milk (any kind)
6 dairy-free probiotic capsules
1 Tbsp. sugar, coconut sugar or maple syrup (the coconut sugar and maple syrup will change the color of the yogurt slightly). The sugar is needed to help with the fermenting process.
2 tsp. agar agar powder (not flakes)

In a saucepan, clip a candy thermometer to the side of the pan. Add the coconut milk, and heat the milk to 180°. Remove from the heat and add the agar powder and sugar, stirring or whisking to dissolve. Let the mixture cool to 90°.

When cooled, open the probiotic capsules contents into a small bowl. Add ½ cup of the cooled milk, and stir or whisk well until the probiotic is dissolved. Add the milk/probiotic mixture back into the remaining milk and stir well.

Pour into a glass container (or yogurt containers), cover and incubate at 90-100° for at least 8 hours *. The mixture will be very runny after incubating. Chill in the refrigerator. The mixture will be very thick at this point. Place the thickened yogurt into a blender and blend until smooth and creamy. A stick blender can also be used instead of a blender.

*To make this, you will need a way to keep the yogurt at a temperature of 90-100° for at least 8 hours. I use a box style dehydrator with a temperature setting. A yogurt maker would also work. If you don't have any of these things, you can fill a crock pot with water that has been heated to 90-100° (you can do this on the stove first), and place your jar sealed tightly in the crock pot on warm/low. You may have to monitor it every few hours, checking the temperature and possibly covering the crock pot with a lid, to make sure it is keeping a warm enough temperature.

Almond Milk Yogurt

1 quart almond milk
1 Tbsp. tapioca flour
1 Tbsp. sugar, coconut sugar or maple syrup
1 tsp. agar agar powder (not flakes)
6 dairy-free probiotic capsules

Place the almond milk and tapioca flour in a saucepan. Whisk well until the tapioca flour is dissolved. Heat the milk mixture to 180°. Remove from the heat and add the agar powder and sugar, stirring or whisking to dissolve. Let the mixture cool to 90°.

When cooled, open the probiotic capsules contents into a small bowl. Add ½ cup of the cooled milk, and stir or whisk well until the probiotic is dissolved. Add the milk/probiotic mixture back into the remaining milk and stir well. Pour into a glass container (or yogurt containers), cover and incubate at 90-100° for at least 8 hours. The mixture will be very runny after incubating. Chill in the refrigerator to thicken. If it becomes very thick, you can make it creamy by blending it with a stick blender.

Yogurt Recipe #3

I wanted to include this very easy way to make yogurt as another option. This recipe calls for a thickener called glucomannan. Because of glucomannan's high fiber content, for some it can cause digestive trouble. I have a very sensitive stomach, and the glucomannan has not bothered me.

1 quart non-dairy milk
1 Tbsp. sugar, coconut sugar or maple syrup
6 probiotic capsules
1 ½ - 2 tsp. glucomannan powder (I used the NOW brand)

Heat the milk in a saucepan to 90°. Stir in the sugar, and stir until dissolved. Place 1 cup of the milk in a small bowl, and open up the probiotic capsules into the milk. Stir well, and add the probiotic milk back into the pan. Stir well.

Place milk in a jar, and incubate for about 8 hours at 90-100°. When you take the mixture out, it may be separated, which is normal. Place in the refrigerator to cool.

Once cold, stir the yogurt (which will probably be separated and runny). Place 1 cup of the yogurt into a blender. Turn the blender on low, and slowly sprinkle the glucomannan into the blender as it is running. Do not dump it in or it will clump, and will not work well. Once sprinkled in, run the blender on high for about 1 minute. Add the thickened mixture to your yogurt and stir well. Place in the refrigerator for several hours to thicken.

Once mixture is thickened, do not stir the yogurt in the jar, as this will make the yogurt runny.

Gluten-Free Sweet Crackers

These are a cross between a cookie and a cracker. They are good by themselves, and do not need anything on them.

2/3 cup almond flour
1/2 cup tapioca flour
1 tsp. xanthan gum
1 Tbsp. Arrowroot powder (or cornstarch)
4 Tbsp. Xylitol or sugar
1/4 tsp. cinnamon
Dash of stevia (use more sugar if you don't like stevia)
1/4 cup coconut oil, melted
2-3 Tbsp. dairy-free milk (or more if needed)

Mix dry ingredients. Mix stevia in with melted coconut oil, and add to dry ingredients. Mix together until crumbly. Add milk and mix well, forming a sticky dough. Press into a pan lined with parchment paper. After pressed, take a knife and cut into squares. Bake at 350° for 15 minutes, or until the crackers are crispy.

Gluten-Free Herb Crackers

2 cups gluten-free flour (rice, garbanzo, or buckwheat)
1½ - 2 cups water (or more, depending on the flour used)
1 tsp. salt (or more to taste)
½ tsp. onion powder
1 tsp. garlic
2 tsp. Italian seasoning

Mix all ingredients together to the consistency of very thin pancake batter. Pour onto an electric griddle or heavily oiled fry pan. Spread the batter out thinly and cook like a pancake*. You want these to be flat. The insides will be on the doughy side. Cool for a few minutes on wire racks. When cool enough to handle, cut with pizza scissors into desired sizes or shapes. Bake on cookie sheets at 300° until crispy. Timing will depend on how thick the crackers are, and the grain used. Turn these a few times as they cook, so that they don't burn, and so that they cook evenly.

*As you are making these pancakes, do a few small ones, and taste them to see if they are to your liking. Add spices of your choice to get the desired flavor.

Maple Corn

Traditional caramel corn is loaded with butter, along with corn syrup and brown sugar. This is a healthier version, and really, really good.

1 cup un-popped popcorn or 8 quarts popped
½ cup coconut oil
1 cup real maple syrup
1 tsp. salt
½ tsp. baking soda
1 tsp. vanilla

Preheat the oven to 250°. Pop the popcorn if it is un-popped. Place popcorn in a very large bowl. In a saucepan, heat the coconut oil, maple syrup and salt until bubbly. Add the baking soda and vanilla, stirring to dissolve the baking soda. Pour over the popcorn and stir well to coat. Divide popcorn evenly in two 9 x 13 pans. Bake for 40-45 minutes, stirring every 15 minutes.

Glazed Nuts

These tasty treats make a great snack. I modified this recipe to make it healthier and with less sugar. Feel free to add regular sugar in place of the xylitol. We make these at Christmas time, or anytime we have a sweet tooth.. A word of warning: these sweet nuts are extremely addictive!

1 ½ cups cashews, almonds, pecans, walnuts, or a mixture of all of these (the nuts can be raw or roasted)
½ cup xylitol or sugar
2 Tbsp. coconut oil
1 tsp. vanilla extract

Cover a baking sheet with aluminum foil, and oil the foil with coconut oil. In a heavy skillet (a cast-iron skillet works well), combine the nuts, xylitol, coconut oil and vanilla. Cook the mixture over medium-high heat. DO NOT STIR. This is very important because the mixture will not harden correctly if you stir it before the sugar starts to melt. Shake the skillet occasionally, until the sugar starts to melt. Reduce the heat to low, and cook, stirring occasionally at this point, until the sugar is a golden brown color.

Pour the cooked nuts onto the oiled baking sheet. Cool completely. Break the nuts into clusters. Store the nuts in an airtight container.

Note: Can be refrigerated to harden, if needed

Fruit Gelatin

Jell-o is gluten-free and dairy-free food, but it is loaded with food coloring, sugar and preservatives. This is a nice alternative.

2 cups 100% fruit juice of your choice (apple, grape, mixed fruit, or whatever you prefer)
3 Tbsp. xylitol, sugar or honey
1 ½ tsp. agar agar powder **
Cut up fruit, fresh or canned (optional) **

In a saucepan, heat juice until hot, but not boiling. Add the agar agar powder and the sugar. Stir well, and bring the mixture to a boil. Reduce the heat, and stir often for 5-6 minutes, or until the sugar and agar agar powder are dissolved. Pour mixture into an 8 x 8 inch pan. Add the fresh or canned fruit to the pan. Chill until the mixture sets.

** I haven't tried the agar agar flakes, but I have read that you can use the flakes in place of the powder. The flakes are double what the powder is, so instead of the 1½ tsp., it would be 1 Tbsp. of the flakes.

** If using canned fruit, make sure it is very well drained. Do not use kiwi or pineapple, as the mixture will not gel.

Tropical Pops

Both grown-ups and kids will love these refreshing, sweet Popsicles made with healthy ingredients. If you don't have Popsicles containers, you can use paper cups with Popsicle sticks.

1 banana
1 can (8 ounces) crushed pineapple, undrained
½ cup casein-free milk
½ tsp. vanilla extract
3 Tbsp. honey or sugar (more, if you want them sweeter)
¼ tsp. liquid stevia (or 3 more Tbsp. sugar, if you want to replace stevia)

Blend all the ingredients in a blender until smooth. Pour into Popsicle containers and freeze.

Fudge Pops

Either carob of cocoa can be used in this recipe. We prefer carob because of the sweeter flavor that carob has, but the cocoa is also good.

2 Tbsp. unsweetened cocoa powder or carob powder
1 Tbsp. cornstarch or arrowroot powder
1/2 cup honey or sugar
½ tsp. liquid stevia (or ½ cup sugar, if you want to replace stevia)
3 cups dairy-free milk
1 tsp. vanilla

In a saucepan, combine the cocoa powder, cornstarch and xylitol. Gradually stir in the milk and stevia, stirring until smooth. Bring to a boil over medium heat and cook and stir for 1-2 minutes, or until slightly thickened. Add vanilla. Cool for 1 hour, stirring occasionally. Pour into Popsicle containers and freeze.

Nachos

I made these for a Super Bowl party at my house. Even those who were able to eat cheese loved these.

1 ½ cup Daiya cheese
½ cup salsa
½ cup dairy-free milk
1 Tbsp. arrowroot or cornstarch
Tortilla chips*

In a saucepan, add the Daiya cheese and salsa. Melt over medium heat until bubbly. In a small bowl, mix the arrowroot with the milk. Add to the pan and stir until thickened. Serve with tortilla chips.

*For corn free tortilla chips, cut grain free tortillas (recipe p.42) into wedges. Place on baking sheets and bake at 350° until crispy.

Mini Pizzas

Grain free tortilla recipe (p. 42)
Pizza or spaghetti sauce
Toppings (green peppers, onions, mushrooms, etc.)
Pepperoni or sausage (optional)
Daiya cheese (optional)

Pour tortillas onto griddle or in a non-stick pan, but do not spread out the batter (you want them to be thicker). Cook like a pancake.

Place cooked mini crusts on cookie sheets. Top with sauce, toppings, meat and cheese. Bake at 350° until cheese is bubbly and toppings are cooked.

* Making the crusts ahead of time and freezing them saves time when making them for lunch or snacks. All that is needed is to thaw the crusts and add the toppings.

Soups, Salads and Side Dishes

Condensed Cream of Celery Soup

So many recipes call for Cream of Celery soup, but the canned soups are usually loaded with gluten, dairy or both. I was very excited to finally get this recipe to work after some failed attempts. This recipe is a great substitute for the store-bought version. I usually quadruple the recipe, and freeze it in jars that are the equivalent of the store bought version. The consistency does change a bit after being frozen, but still works well in recipes. This soup also tastes great by itself, with a sandwich or salad.

4 cups chopped celery
2/3 cup chopped onions
¼ cup olive oil
2 tsp. salt
1/8 tsp. pepper
1 tsp. dried parsley
4 cups water
3 Tbsp. tapioca flour
1 cup dairy-free milk

Heat olive oil in a Dutch oven. Sauté the onions and celery in olive oil until they are translucent. Stir in the salt, pepper, parsley and water. Simmer for about 30 minutes, then remove from the heat and cool slightly.
Place all ingredients in a blender and process until smooth. Return the mixture to the pan and bring to a boil. Mix tapioca flour into the milk, making sure there are no lumps. Add the milk mixture to the pan, and cook and stir until the mixture thickens.

**This makes about one quart of condensed soup. Store-bought condensed soup cans are 10.5 ounces, or roughly 1¼ cups of soup. This recipe makes the equivalent of 3 cans of store-bought condensed soup.

Condensed Cream of Chicken Soup

My friend Andrew Cordova has come up with some amazing gluten free recipes. He has a very active Facebook page called Gluten Free Recipes for Celiacs, where he posts recipes, ideas and information to those who cannot have gluten. I am grateful to him for allowing me to use one of his recipes in my book. I use this recipe in casseroles all the time. It is quick and easy, and very tasty.

½ cup chicken broth
½ cup dairy-free milk
2 Tbsp. ghee or casein-free margarine
1/8 tsp. onion powder
1/8 tsp. garlic powder
1/8 tsp. pepper
1/8 tsp. salt
1/8 tsp. parsley
1 1/2 Tbsp. potato starch (arrowroot also works)

In a medium saucepan melt ghee or margarine. Pour in chicken broth and milk. Add onion powder, garlic powder, pepper, salt, parsley. Increase heat to medium high and bring to a boil for 2 minutes. Turn off heat and slowly whisk in potato starch.

Carrot Salad

2 cups chopped carrots
¼ cup raisins
1/3 cup mayonnaise
2 Tbsp. dairy free milk
1 Tbsp. honey

Combine raisins and carrots together in a bowl. In a small bowl, mix mayo, milk and honey until well blended. The dressing should be runny. Pour over the carrots and raisins and mix well.

Quinoa Tabouleh

2 cups dry quinoa
2 cucumbers, peeled, seeded and chopped
2 large tomatoes, or 4 Roma tomatoes, seeded and chopped
3 Tablespoons dried minced onion
1/2 cup chopped cilantro
1 small can sliced black olives
3/4 cup olive oil
Juice of 2 large lemons, or 3 small lemons
2 1/2 tsp. salt, or to taste

If possible, soak the quinoa at room temperature with 2 tsp. of lemon juice overnight. This helps make the quinoa easier to digest. This step is not necessary, just helpful for those with digestive problems. If you soak the quinoa overnight, drain and rinse before cooking. If you do not soak the quinoa, make sure to rinse it well before you cook it. Place the quinoa in a large pan, and add 4 cups of water. Bring quinoa to a boil, and turn the heat down to simmer. Cover with a lid, and cook for 20 minutes, or until quinoa is cooked through and the water is gone. Remove from heat and allow quinoa to cool.

Once quinoa is cooled, add the cucumbers, tomatoes, dried onions, cilantro and black olives in a large bowl. In a separate bowl, mix the olive oil, lemon juice and salt. Add to the quinoa mixture and mix well. Refrigerate for at least 1 hour to allow flavors to marinate.

**This recipe makes a very large amount. Recipe can be cut in half.

Berry Tossed Salad

6 cups chopped lettuce
1 ½ c. fresh strawberries, sliced
1 medium onion, sliced and separated into rings
¼ c. slivered almonds

Dressing:
½ c. olive oil
3 Tbsp. lemon juice
¼ tsp. garlic powder
¼ tsp. onion powder
¼ tsp. liquid stevia
3 Tbsp. honey (double the honey amount if you do not want to use stevia)
¼ tsp. salt
¼ tsp. dried mustard

Toss the salad ingredients together. Mix the dressing ingredients in a jar, and mix well. Serve the dressing with the salad.

Quinoa Pilaf

This is a family favorite, and a great side dish with chicken or steak. You could try replacing the quinoa for rice, if you do not care for quinoa.

1 medium onion, chopped
1 clove garlic, minced
½ cup chopped celery
2 tsp. oil
½ cup green peppers
½ cup chopped carrots
2 ½ cups chicken broth
1 tsp. salt
1 cup quinoa, rinsed*

In a medium saucepan, cook the onion, garlic and celery in oil until the onions are transparent. Add the green peppers, carrots, chicken broth, and salt. Bring it to a boil, and stir in the quinoa. Return to a boil. Reduce heat, cover and simmer for 20 minutes, or until liquid is absorbed, stirring occasionally.

*Quinoa is easier to digest if it is soaked. To soak, cover the dry quinoa with water and add 1 Tablespoon lemon juice. Cover and place on the counter for 6-8 hours. Drain and rinse, then cook as you normally would.

Zucchini Rounds

My husband's family always called these Zucchini Rounds, but they are actually Zucchini Pancakes. The original recipe for this was a family recipe that had been passed down two generations. It had wheat and Parmesan cheese, which made them taste wonderful. This modified recipe is a nice alternative. Besides just eating them as a side dish, I like to use them as hamburger buns or as bread for meat sandwiches.

3 slices regular bacon or turkey bacon **
1/4 cup tapioca flour
1/4 cup gluten free flour (millet, rice, garbanzo, etc.)
2 tsp. baking powder
½ tsp. salt
1/4 tsp. onion powder
1/4 tsp. garlic powder
1 Tbsp. oil
2 eggs
2 cups zucchini, shredded (yellow squash will also work)

Cook bacon. Break the bacon up into small pieces. In a mixing bowl, add the bacon, tapioca flour, gluten-free flour blend, baking powder, salt, onion powder, garlic powder, oil and eggs. Fold in zucchini. Spoon onto a griddle or heavily oiled fry pan, and spread the batter out a little, making a pancake. Cook like regular pancakes. Enjoy with ketchup.

**Note: Oscar Meyer's regular bacon and turkey bacon is GFCF, but contains nitrates/nitrites. Applegate Farms has regular bacon and turkey bacon that is GFCF, and is free of nitrates/nitrites. Hormel Real Bacon Bits can also be used (2-3 Tbsp.) in place of the bacon.

Sweet Potato Fries

These are great with burgers, or with meatloaf. They are a nice change from traditional fries, and are a healthier alternative.

2-3 large sweet potatoes
2 Tbsp. olive oil
Salt to taste
Garlic to taste

Preheat oven to 375°. Peel the sweet potatoes, and cut them into slices that are about ¼ inch thick. If you prefer to do them in a fry shape, you can do that instead. Place the cut up fries in a large Ziplock bag with the oil. Seal and shake well to coat the potatoes.

Place the potatoes on cookie sheets, making sure not to overlap the potatoes. Sprinkle with salt and garlic. Bake, turning every 15 minutes to make sure they don't burn*. Towards the end of the baking, watch them closely because they can burn easily.

These are great with ketchup!

*I didn't include an actual cooking time on these because it all depends on how thick they are sliced (or if they are fry-shaped). Normally they take me about 30-45 minutes.

Speedy Spuds

My Mom made these often when I was a kid, and they were one of my favorite side dishes. I modified them so my family could continue to enjoy them.

¼ cup ghee or casein-free margarine
Potatoes
Salt
Garlic

Preheat oven to 450°. Place the ghee or casein-free margarine in a 9 x 13 inch baking pan and place in the oven to melt. Scrub potatoes, but do not peel. Slice the potatoes into ¾ inch slices, and add them to the ghee/margarine, turning to coat. Sprinkle the potatoes with salt and garlic.

Bake for 30 minutes, turning once. After the 30 minutes, turn the oven to broil. Broil the potatoes until they are crisp and brown on the outside, and tender on the inside.

Mashed Potato Cakes

1 Tbsp. dried minced onions
2 eggs
1/3 cup gluten-free flour
½ tsp. garlic powder
1 tsp. salt
¼ tsp. pepper
2 cups mashed potatoes
1 Tbsp. oil

Mix all ingredients together. Drop the mixture onto a griddle or heavily oiled fry pan and flatten slightly. Cook until browned on each side. Serve with ketchup.

Spiced Carrot Strips

5 large carrots, julienned
2 Tbsp. ghee or casein-free margarine, melted
1 Tbsp. honey
1 tsp. salt
½ tsp. ground cinnamon

Cook carrots in a saucepan or steamer until tender. Drain. Combine the ghee or margarine, honey, salt and cinnamon. Pour over the carrots and toss to coat. Serve immediately.

Candied Sweet Potatoes

My Grandmother used to make the most wonderful candied sweet potatoes every year for Thanksgiving. When she passed away many years ago, I wanted to continue with her tradition of making candied sweet potatoes. I modified her recipe to make it GFCFSF friendly. When I made it for the first time last Thanksgiving, I was happy to see that no one seemed to notice the difference.

3 large sweet potatoes or yams
½ cup water
½ cup coconut sugar (or packed brown sugar)
¼ tsp. liquid stevia (or another ½ cup packed brown sugar)
2 Tbsp. ghee or casein-free margarine
1/8 cup real maple syrup

Cook sweet potatoes/yams until soft (steaming works well, and is fast). In a saucepan, add the water, sugar, stevia (if adding), and ghee or margarine, and maple syrup. Bring to a boil. Place cut up sweet potatoes in a baking dish, and pour the hot syrup over the potatoes.

Bake at 350° for 50-60 minutes, basting every 15 minutes.

Mashed "Faux-tatoes"

I am always trying to find ways to get my family to eat more vegetables. This is a nice change from traditional mashed potatoes. They are tasty enough to fool even the picky eaters into thinking they are eating mashed potatoes.

1 package (16 ounce) frozen cauliflower, or 1 small head of fresh cauliflower
2 pieces bacon or 2 Tbsp. real bacon bits
1 Tbsp. ghee or casein-free margarine
Salt to taste

Cook bacon and let cool. Cook cauliflower until soft. Place the cauliflower and bacon in a blender or food processor and process until smooth**. Do not add water unless absolutely necessary because the mixture will be too watery. Return the mix to a saucepan. Add the ghee or margarine, and salt to taste. Serve hot.

**A stick blender would work for this recipe.

**Note: This recipe does not make a large amount, so the recipe can be doubled.

Main Dishes

Shake-N-Bake Chicken

I have used many different kinds of gluten-free flours for this recipe, and all have tasted good. Experiment and see which you prefer.

2-3 pounds chicken pieces
½ cup gluten-free flour
1 ½ tsp. salt
1 tsp. paprika
1 tsp. garlic
1 tsp. onion powder
¼ tsp. pepper
¼ tsp. ground sage
1/3 cup ghee or casein-free margarine

Preheat oven to 350°. Melt the ghee or margarine in a 8 ½ x 11 inch pan, or a 9 x 13 inch pan if using more chicken. Put the flour and spices in a Ziplock bag. Shake well to mix the ingredients together. Add the chicken pieces a little at a time and shake well. Place chicken, skin side down, in pan. Bake for 30 minutes, then turn the chicken and bake another 30 minutes, or until chicken is cooked all the way through.

Makeover Meatloaf

I like to freeze spaghetti sauce in ice cube trays, so that when I need a little for a recipe, I can thaw a few cubes out. I do that for this recipe, and it makes it a quick and easy.

1 pound ground beef
1 egg, beaten
1/8 cup chopped onion
½ tsp. salt
½ tsp. garlic powder
2 Tbsp. spaghetti sauce
¼ cup chopped green peppers
¼ cup spaghetti sauce (for the top)

Preheat oven to 350°. Combine the egg, onion, salt, garlic powder and 2 tablespoons spaghetti sauce in a bowl. Mix well to combine. Add the ground beef and the chopped green peppers. Mix well to combine all the ingredients. Place in a greased loaf pan and bake for 45 minutes. Top with ¼ cup spaghetti sauce. Bake for another 15 minutes.

Tuna Chowder

When I first saw this recipe from an old family cookbook, I was curious as to how it would taste. After adapting it, it reminds me a little bit of clam chowder. It is good for those cold winter days.

1 large onion, chopped
1 Tbsp. oil
1 cup chopped celery
2 medium carrots, diced
1 cup diced potatoes
2 cups water
1 (7 ounce) can tuna, drained
3 cups dairy-free milk, divided
1 tsp. salt or more to taste
1/8 tsp. pepper
1 tsp. garlic powder
1 tsp. dried parsley
3 Tbsp. arrowroot powder or cornstarch

Cook onion in oil until tender. Add celery, carrots, potatoes and water. Bring to a boil, cover and simmer until veggies are tender. Add tuna, 2 ½ cups milk, salt, pepper, garlic powder and parsley. Bring to a boil. In a bowl, mix the remaining ½ cup milk with the arrowroot or cornstarch. Pour into the soup. Cook and stir until thickened.

Creamy Chicken and Rice Soup

1 cup carrots, sliced thinly
1 large onion, chopped
½ cup chopped green peppers
1 cup chopped celery
2 Tbsp. olive oil
2 cans (14 ounces each) chicken broth
1½ cups cooked rice
1½ cups cooked chicken
1-2 tsp. salt, or to taste
¼ tsp. pepper
½ tsp. onion powder
1 tsp. garlic
1 Tbsp. cooking wine (optional)
1 cup dairy-free milk
2 Tbsp. arrowroot or cornstarch

Sauté the onions in olive oil until translucent. Add carrots, green pepper, and celery and sauté for 2 minutes. Add the chicken broth, rice, chicken, salt, pepper, onion powder and garlic powder. Bring to a boil. Cover and cook for 10-15 minutes, or until veggies are tender. Mix milk with cornstarch or arrowroot. Pour into the soup. Add the cooking wine. Cook and stir until thickened.

Baked Ziti

This recipe makes a large amount, and freezes well. I have made this for family gatherings, and when friends have come over, and they didn't know it was gluten-free!

16 ounces gluten-free ziti pasta (spirals can also be used)
1 pound ground beef
1 cup chopped onion
2 cloves garlic, minced
1 tsp. basil
1 tsp. oregano
3 cups spaghetti sauce
Casein-free cheese (like Daiya brand), optional

Cook ziti according to package. Set aside. Brown ground beef with onion and garlic. Drain. Add basil, oregano, and spaghetti sauce. Add ground beef mixture to pasta. Mix well.

Place in a greased 9 x 13 inch baking pan. Cover with aluminum foil. Bake at 350° for 20 minutes. Uncover and add cheese (if using), and bake uncovered for another 10 minutes.

Slow Cooker Curried Chicken

2-3 pounds chicken pieces
1 tsp. salt
1/8 tsp. pepper
1 cup chicken broth
2 Tbsp. ghee or casein-free margarine, melted
1 Tbsp. dried minced onion
2 tsp. curry powder
2 garlic cloves, minced

Place chicken in a slow cooker. In a bowl, add the remaining ingredients and mix well. Pour over the chicken.

Cover and cook on low for 4-5 hours, or until chicken is cooked through.

Chicken-A-La-King

1 Tbsp. ghee or casein-free margarine
1 medium onion, chopped
1 cup chicken broth
1 cup dairy-free milk, divided
1 cup chopped green peppers
1 cup frozen peas (optional)
½ - 1 tsp. salt, or to taste
1/8 tsp. pepper
½ tsp. onion powder
½ tsp. garlic powder
2 Tbsp. arrowroot powder or cornstarch
2 cups cooked chicken

Cook onion in ghee or margarine until tender. Add the broth and ¾ cup milk. Bring to a boil. Add the green peppers, peas, salt, pepper, onion powder and garlic powder. Bring back to a boil. In a small bowl, mix the remaining ¼ cup milk with the arrowroot or cornstarch. Add to the pan. Cook and stir until thickened. Add the cooked chicken, and heat through.

Serve over rice, biscuits, toast, pasta or mashed potatoes.

Stuffed Peppers

The stuffing for this makes quite a bit. I like to freeze it in small portions, so that I can make a quick meal.

2 cups water
1 cup uncooked rice (white or brown)
3 large bell peppers, halved and seeded
1 pound ground beef
1 large onion, diced
1 tsp. garlic
½ tsp. chili powder
½ tsp. oregano
½ tsp. cumin
Salt and pepper to taste
1 can (15 ounces) tomato sauce—use more if needed
Shredded casein-free cheese, optional

Cook rice with water, according to directions. Brown the ground beef with the onion in a Dutch oven. Add the rice and spices. Pour in the tomato sauce and mix thoroughly. Let the mixture simmer for about 10 minutes. Remove from the heat. Spoon the mixture onto each half of the green pepper, and place on a greased baking pan. Bake at 350° for 40-45 minutes or until golden brown. Sprinkle with cheese, if using, and bake for another 5-10 minutes until cheese is melted and lightly browned.

Shepherds Pie

If you have leftover mashed potatoes, this recipe is a great way to use them up. Mashed potato flakes can also be used. We make this recipe for St. Patrick's Day, along with Irish Soda Bread.

1 pound ground beef
1 onion, chopped
1½ cups drained stewed tomatoes
1 tsp. parsley flakes
½ tsp. garlic powder
¼ tsp. pepper
½ tsp. salt
2-3 cups mashed potatoes
¼ cup shredded casein-free cheese, optional
1 Tbsp. ghee or casein-free margarine

Brown the meat and onions. Add the tomatoes, parsley flakes, garlic powder, pepper, and salt. Mix well. Pour into a casserole dish (I use a 2 quart round dish). Spread the mashed potatoes over the top. Sprinkle cheese, if using, on the top, and dot the mashed potatoes with the ghee or margarine. Bake at 350° for 30 minutes.

Crustless Quiche

3-4 slices cooked bacon, 2-3 Tbsp. real bacon pieces, or ½ - 1 cup ham, cubed
1 cup fresh or frozen chopped broccoli or spinach (if using frozen, thaw it first)
1 small onion, chopped
½ cup gluten-free flour blend (p. 32)
½ tsp. baking powder
1 tsp. salt
1/8 tsp. pepper
½ tsp. garlic powder
1 Tbsp. ghee or casein-free margarine
3 eggs
1½ cups dairy-free milk

Preheat oven to 350°. Line the bottom of a greased pie plate or 2 quart casserole dish with the meat and the vegetables. In a blender, add onion, gluten-free flour blend, baking powder, salt, pepper, garlic, ghee or margarine, eggs and milk. Blend until smooth. Pour over the meat/veggie mixture.

Bake for 45-55 minutes, or until a knife inserted near center comes out clean.

Tater-Tot Casserole

We do not eat tater-tots very often in our house, but I do make this as a treat once in a while.

1 pound ground beef, seasoned with salt, pepper and garlic, cooked and drained
1 ¼ cup condensed cream of celery soup or cream of chicken soup (p. 61 or 62)
½ cup dairy-free milk
16 ounces gluten-free tater tots (Ore-Ida are gluten free)
Peas or green beans, optional
Casein-free cheese (like Daiya), optional

Place cooked meat in the bottom of a casserole dish and place a layer of optional peas or green beans on top, if using. Add a layer of tater tots. Mix soup and milk. Pour over the top of the tater tots. Sprinkle with optional cheese. Bake at 350° for 20-30 minutes.

Salmonettes

I have used several different kinds of flours for this, and all have worked well. Even quinoa worked. The salmon was strong enough to mask the flavor.

1 can salmon (14 ¾ oz.)
1 egg, lightly beaten
½ cup gluten-free flour (rice, garbanzo, etc.)
½ tsp. xanthan gum
¼ tsp. dill weed
1 tsp. onion powder
½ tsp. salt
2 tsp. baking powder
¼ cup dairy-free milk

Drain salmon and discard bones and skins. In a bowl, combine all ingredients. Drop batter by ¼ cupfuls onto skillet heated with oil. Cook until golden brown, turning several times.

Serve with mustard or tartar sauce

Creamy Chicken Over Rice

4 cups frozen California blend vegetables
¼ cup water
1 ¼ c. condensed cream of celery or cream of chicken soup (p. 61 or p. 62)
2 cups cooked chicken
½ tsp. salt, or to taste
½ tsp. garlic
Hot cooked rice

Put frozen vegetables and water in a saucepan. Cook vegetables until tender. Add the soup, chicken, salt and garlic to the pan. Cook until heated through. Serve over hot rice.

Chicken and Biscuits

Biscuits:
1 ½ cups gluten-free flour blend (p. 32)
1 Tbsp. baking powder
1 tsp. xanthan gum
2 tsp. sugar or xylitol
½ tsp. cream of tartar
½ tsp. salt
¼ cup olive oil
¾ cup dairy-free milk

Preheat oven to 350°. In a bowl, combine flour, baking powder, xanthan gum, sugar, cream of tartar and salt. Add oil and mix until it resembles coarse crumbs. Add milk and stir until just moistened. Drop onto greased baking sheet. Bake for 15-20 minutes.

Cream Sauce:
1 small onion, chopped
1 Tbsp. oil
½ - 1 tsp. salt, or to taste
1/8 tsp. pepper
1 cup dairy-free milk, divided
1 cup chicken broth
2 cups cooked chicken
1 ½ cups frozen peas
2 ½ Tbsp. arrowroot powder or cornstarch

Cook the onion in oil until tender. Add the salt, pepper, ½ cup milk and all the chicken broth. Add the chicken and peas. Cook until peas are done. Mix remaining ½ cup milk with the arrowroot or cornstarch. Add to the pot. Cook and stir until thickened.

Serve cream sauce over biscuits.

Hearty Chicken Casserole

8 ounces gluten-free pasta (elbows or spirals)
1 Tbsp. oil
1 small onion, chopped
1 cup dairy-free milk, divided
2 cups chicken broth
½ - 1 tsp. salt (or to taste)
1/8 tsp. pepper
½ tsp. garlic powder
½ tsp. onion powder
½ tsp. basil
2 cups peas or mixed vegetables
2 cups cooked chicken
3 Tbsp. arrowroot powder or cornstarch

Cook pasta according to directions. In a large saucepan, cook onion in oil. Add ½ cup milk, the chicken broth, salt, pepper, garlic powder, onion powder and basil. Add peas or mixed vegetables and chicken, and cook until the vegetables are tender. In a small bowl, mix arrowroot or cornstarch with the remaining ½ cup milk. Add milk mixture to the chicken mixture and cook until thickened. Add pasta and stir well to combine ingredients. Pour into a 9 x 13 inch pan or into a casserole dish. Bake at 350° for 20 minutes.

Honey-Mustard Chicken

2-4 pounds chicken pieces (legs, thighs, wings, etc.)
¼ cup spicy mustard
¼ cup regular mustard
½ cup honey
1/3 cup olive oil
2 Tbsp. lemon juice

Place chicken in a pan. Combine remaining ingredients in a saucepan and bring to a boil. Pour over chicken and bake at 350° for 1 hour, or until chicken is done, turning once.

Mexican Chicken

2-3 pounds chicken pieces (legs, wings, thighs, or a mixture)
1/3 cup gluten-free flour of choice
1/3 cup cornmeal*
1 Tbsp. ground cumin
1 ½ tsp. salt
1/8 tsp. pepper (more if you like it spicy)
¾ tsp. cayenne pepper (omit if you don't like spicy food)

Preheat oven to 350°. In a large re-sealable plastic bag, add all of the dry ingredients. Shake well to combine ingredients, then add the chicken pieces to the bag and shake to coat. Place coated chicken pieces in a greased baking dish. Bake for 55-60 minutes, or until chicken is done, turning once.

*Millet flour can be used in place of the cornmeal

BBQ Grilled Chicken

This is an old family recipe that has very good flavor. It tastes best when grilled, but can also be baked in the oven.

½ cup olive oil
1 cup white vinegar
1 Tbsp. salt
1 ½ tsp. poultry seasoning
1 tsp. pepper
1 egg, beaten
2-3 pounds or more of chicken

In a large bowl, mix all ingredients except chicken. Stir well to combine ingredients. Add chicken pieces, and cover the bowl. Place in the refrigerator, and marinate for 6-8 hours or more.

Grill chicken, basting with the marinade. You can also bake in the oven at 350° until chicken is cooked.

Deviled Chicken

4 Tbsp. ghee or casein-free margarine, melted
1 Tbsp. prepared mustard (not dried)
1 Tbsp. lemon juice
1 tsp. salt
½ tsp. garlic
¼ tsp. pepper
1 tsp. paprika
5-6 chicken legs or thighs

Preheat oven to 350°. Place chicken in a greased baking dish. In a bowl, add remaining ingredients and mix well. Pour over the chicken. Bake for 60 minutes, basting twice during baking.

Pour Pizza

This easy recipe got its name because it has a crust that you can pour, instead of having to roll the crust out.

1 pound ground beef
1 onion, chopped
1 tsp. salt, divided
¼ tsp. pepper
1 cup gluten-free flour (rice or garbanzo work well)
1 tsp. oregano or Italian seasoning
2 eggs
2/3 cup dairy-free milk
2 cups spaghetti or pizza sauce
Casein-free cheese (like Daiya)
Black olives, green peppers, mushrooms, and/or whatever toppings you prefer

In a skillet, brown the ground beef with the onion. Season the meat with ½ tsp. salt and the ¼ tsp. pepper. Set aside. In a mixing bowl, combine the flour, oregano or Italian seasoning, eggs and milk. Stir to form a smooth batter. Pour into a greased 9 x 13 pan, and crumble the meat mixture over the batter. Bake at 375° for 20-25 minutes (crust will bubble up a bit).

Remove from oven and spoon the spaghetti or pizza sauce over the crust. Add toppings, and sprinkle with cheese, if using. Return to the oven and bake for another 20 minutes, or until cheese if melted.

Italian Beef

1 large onion, sliced and quartered
3½ - 4 pounds roast
½ - 1 cup water
1¾ tsp. dried basil
1 ½ tsp. garlic powder
1½ tsp. oregano
1¼ tsp. salt
¼ tsp. pepper

Mix spices together. Cut up the meat into smaller chunks. In a slow cooker, layer meat and onion, then add some of the spices. Layer again, adding the spices after the layer. Continue layering until the meat and spices are used up. Pour water gently over the top. Cook on low for 8-9 hours. Add more water as the roast cooks, if needed.

Can be eaten as a roast, or shredded and served on sandwiches.

Salisbury Steak

1 pound ground beef
1 egg, lightly beaten
1 Tbsp. dried minced onion
¼ cup gluten-free cracker crumbs or bread crumbs**
½ tsp. garlic powder
½ tsp. salt
1/8 tsp. pepper

In a bowl, combine all ingredients. Cover the bowl and refrigerate for 1-2 hours, to allow flavors to mingle. Form into oval shaped patties, and cook like hamburgers.

**To make your own bread crumbs, toast gluten-free bread. Pulverize toasted bread in a blender or food processor until fine.

Calzones

Calzones are like folded over pizzas. I found gluten-free calzones in a mix at our grocery store, but they were really expensive. It motivated me to come up with my own recipe.

1 cup almond flour
1 ½ cups gluten-free flour blend (p. 32)
1 tsp. garlic
1 Tbsp. Italian seasoning
1 tsp. salt
2 tsp. xanthan gum
1 tsp. sugar
½ cup dairy-free milk
2 eggs
¼ cup olive oil
½ cup tapioca flour (or more)
Spaghetti or pizza sauce
Toppings of choice such as sausage, pepperoni, green peppers, mushrooms, olives

In a large bowl, combine the almond flour, gluten-free flour blend, garlic, Italian seasoning, salt, xanthan gum, and sugar, mixing well to combine. In a separate bowl, mix the eggs, olive oil and milk, then add the egg mixture to the dry ingredients. Mix until the dough is wet. Start adding the tapioca flour to the dough until the dough can be kneaded. Divide the dough into 4 equal parts. Flatten each part on greased cookie sheets, into four roughly 8 inch pizzas.

Put sauce and toppings of choice onto ½ of each pizza, being careful not to put sauce too near the edges. Fold dough in half over filling and seal edges with fingers or fork. Prick the top, and brush with olive oil and sprinkle with a little salt and garlic.

Bake at 350° for 30-40 minutes until crusts are golden brown.

Tastes Like Port-A-Pit Chicken

This recipe is a variation from the first BBQ recipe, and has a taste like Port-A-Pit chicken. I have only grilled this chicken, but it probably could be put in the oven also.

1½ cups white vinegar
1½ cups water
¾ cups olive oil
2 Tbsp. salt
2 ½ Tbsp. Worcestershire sauce (Lea and Perrins is gluten free)
½ - 1 Tbsp. black pepper
½ Tbsp. garlic powder
½ Tbsp. celery salt
½ Tbsp. paprika
½ Tbsp. onion powder
½ Tbsp. chili powder
2-3 pounds of chicken

Mix all the ingredients minus the chicken in a bowl and stir well. Place chicken pieces in a bowl. Cover the bowl and put in the refrigerator to marinate. Marinate for several hours before grilling.

When grilling, use marinade to baste with during cooking.

Cajun Burgers

1 pound ground beef
1 Tbsp. dried minced onions or ¼ cup finely chopped onion
½ tsp. cumin
½ tsp. oregano
½ tsp. garlic powder
½ tsp. salt
1/8 tsp. cayenne pepper (more if you like it spicy, or omit if you don't like spicy)
¼ tsp. basil

Combine all ingredients and shape into patties. Pan fry or grill.

Chicken Italiano

4 boneless chicken breasts
2 cups tomato sauce
1 tsp. salt
1 tsp. dried parsley
¼ tsp. pepper
1 tsp. Italian seasoning
½ tsp. oregano

Place chicken in a baking dish. In a saucepan, combine remaining ingredients and bring to a boil. Pour over chicken and bake at 350° for 45 minutes to 1 hour, depending on the thickness of the chicken.

Before serving, cut chicken into pieces and pour sauce over the top.

Southwestern Goulash

1 cup uncooked gluten-free elbow macaroni
1 pound ground beef
1 small onion, chopped
1 can (28 ounces) diced tomatoes, drained
1 cup salsa (mild or hot)
½ tsp. ground cumin
1/8 tsp. pepper
½ tsp. salt (or more to taste)

Cook macaroni according to package directions. While pasta is cooking, in a Dutch oven, cook beef and onion until meat is no longer pink; drain. Stir in the diced tomatoes, salsa, cumin, pepper and salt. Bring to a boil. Reduce heat; simmer, uncovered for 3-4 minutes or until heated through.

Drain macaroni and add to meat mixture. Heat through.

Tuna Burgers

1 can (6 ounces) tuna, drained
1 egg
1/3 cup finely chopped onion or 1 Tbsp. dried minced onion
¼ cup finely chopped celery
¼ cup chopped red or green pepper
½ cup gluten-free bread crumbs**
¼ tsp. oregano
¼ tsp. dill weed
¼ tsp. salt
1/8 tsp. pepper
1 tsp. onion powder
¼ cup mayonnaise

Add all ingredients together in a bowl. Drop by large spoonfuls onto griddle or well-oiled fry pan. Flatten slightly with a spoon to make a patty. Flip a few times during cooking.

Serve with mustard or tartar sauce.

**To make your own bread crumbs, toast gluten-free bread. Pulverize in a blender or food processor until fine.

Baked Chicken Nuggets

My daughter loves chicken nuggets, but most have both gluten and dairy in them along with soy. There are GFCFSF chicken nuggets on the market, but they are really expensive. Plus, they are all fried. I wanted to come up with a recipe that was both healthy and tasty. These passed the test with my family! This recipe can easily be doubled.

1 cup gluten-free flour
1 tsp. salt
¼ tsp. pepper
1 tsp. onion powder
1 tsp. garlic powder
1 egg, beaten
1 pound boneless chicken breast cut into 1 inch cubes
Oil for baking pan

In a medium-sized bowl, add the flour, salt, pepper, onion powder, and garlic powder. Mix well to combine. Place egg in a small bowl and beat. Dip the chicken pieces in egg, and then in the flour mixture. Place the chicken pieces in a heavily oiled baking pan and bake for 20 minutes. Turn the pieces and bake for another 15-20 minutes more, or until golden brown and crispy.

Quinoa Pizza Bites
These can be used as a main dish or an appetizer.

2 cups cooked quinoa
2 large eggs
1 cup chopped onion
1 cup Daiya Cheese (optional)
1/2 tsp. garlic powder
2 Tbsp. dried basil (it sounds like a lot, but it adds great flavor)
1 cup pepperoni slices, chopped into pieces (about 1/2 of a 6 ounce bag)
1/2 tsp. seasoned salt (I make my own to avoid food coloring and gluten)
1 tsp. paprika
1 tsp. oregano
Pizza sauce for dipping (I used homemade spaghetti sauce)

Mix together all ingredients except pizza sauce. Fill greased mini muffin tin cups to the top of each cup, pressing down gently to compact. Bake at 350 degrees for 20-25 minutes. Serve with pizza sauce.

Mini Chicken Pot Pies

1 cup gluten free flour (I used garbanzo)
1 tsp. salt
4 tsp. baking powder
2 T. oil
1 c. milk
4 eggs
1 tsp. basil
1 tsp. garlic
Veggies of choice like carrots, peas, onions, etc.
Chicken or whatever meat you want **
Daiya cheese (optional)

Preheat oven to 350 degrees. Mix the first 8 ingredients in a bowl. In a sprayed muffin pan, add 1 tablespoon of the mix into each muffin cup. Add veggies, meat and cheese. Top with another 1-2 tablespoons (depending on how much room you have left) mix. Bake for 30-40 minutes, or until they test done. Remove immediately from pan onto wire rack. Serve warm.

**Another idea for this is to make a pizza type mini pie. Use veggies like onions, green peppers, black olives, etc., and use pepperoni or sausage as the meat. After cooking, top with pizza sauce and cheese, and bake again just long enough to melt the cheese.

Pop-Over Pizza

1 lb. ground beef or ground turkey
1 large onion, chopped
1 green pepper, chopped
2 c. spaghetti sauce
1 small can sliced black olives
1 c. pepper jack Daiya cheese (optional)
2 eggs
1 c. dairy-free milk
1 Tbsp. olive oil
1 Tbsp. baking powder
¾ c. garbanzo flour
¼ c. tapioca flour
1 tsp. basil
1 tsp. salt
1 tsp. garlic

Brown the meat in a skillet, along with the onion and green pepper. Drain. Stir in the spaghetti sauce, and simmer for 5 minutes. Add the black olives, and spoon the mixture into a greased 9 x 13 inch pan. Top with optional pepper jack cheese.

Beat eggs, milk and olive oil until well blended. Add remaining ingredients and mix well. Pour over meat mixture and spread to cover. Bake at 350° for 25-30 minutes, or until the pizza is cooked through.

Sweet Barbecue Chicken

½ c. ketchup
½ c. all fruit jelly (grape works well for this)
1 Tbsp. Worcestershire sauce (Lea and Perrins is GF)
1 Tbsp. dried onion
½ tsp. salt
2 c. cooked chicken, cut into small chunks *
GFCF hamburger buns

Mix the ketchup, jelly, Worcestershire, onion and salt in a saucepan. Slowly bring to a boil, and add the cooked chicken. Heat through. Serve on hamburger buns.

*Cooked turkey would also work for this recipe

Grandma's Chicken and Rice

I modified this recipe from a recipe that was passed down from my grandmother, who was a wonderful cook. The original recipe was one of my favorites as a child. The modified version is just as tasty!

1 c. brown rice or white rice (more can be added)
Chicken pieces
1 recipe Condensed Cream of Chicken Soup (p. 62)
1 c. water (more if using more rice)
3 Tbsp. dried minced onion
1 tsp. onion powder
1 tsp. salt

Preheat oven to 350°. Spread dry rice in a greased 9 x 13 pan, adding more if desired. Place chicken pieces on top of the rice. Mix soup with the water (add more water if adding more rice), dried onion, onion powder and salt. Pour over chicken and rice.

Cover and bake for 1 ½ hours for brown rice or 1 hour for white rice. Take cover off for 15 minutes to let brown.

Desserts

Fruit Ice Cream

When I started trying to eat healthier many years ago, I wanted ice cream! This actually is a really tasty alternative, and has the consistency of ice cream. Plus it is healthy!

Frozen bananas, frozen mangos or frozen strawberries
Dairy-free milk
Vanilla
Sweetener of choice

If you have a high powered blender (like a Vitamix), place ingredients in and blend until smooth. Make sure you do not over-blend, or you will have a smoothie! If you do not have a high-powered blender, you can use a stick blender for this. Place frozen fruit in a re-sealable plastic bag and seal. Pound the frozen fruit with a hammer, or with the smooth side of a meat tenderizer until the fruit is flattened (this will make blending easier). Place pounded fruit in a mixing bowl, and let sit for a few minutes to soften so that it isn't rock solid. Add a small amount of milk, along with some vanilla and sweetener. Start blending with an immersion/stick blender, and add more milk if needed until it is a soft, creamy consistency. Serve immediately.

**Note: I have only made this with a stick blender and a Vitamix. It should work with a regular blender as well. Just make sure to stop the blender often and scrape the sides.

**One really yummy treat is to add peanut butter (if allowed) with the bananas when blending.

Mint Chip Ice Cream

This takes a little bit of preparation, but the taste is worth it! You will not taste the spinach or chlorophyll. It gives the ice cream its color.

3 cups coconut milk (I used homemade)
½ cup fresh spinach, 1 Tablespoon frozen spinach, or ½ tsp. liquid chlorophyll
2-3 drops food grade peppermint oil (I used Young Living)
Stevia to taste (or whatever sweetener you prefer)
Chocolate chips or a broken up chocolate bar (I used one of my homemade chocolate bars from p. 127 and broke the bar into pieces)

Blend the milk, spinach (or chlorophyll), peppermint oil and sweetener in a blender until smooth. If there are small pieces of spinach after blending, strain the milk through a very fine mesh strainer. Pour into ice cube trays or a shallow container. Freeze.

Once frozen, pop the frozen milk cubes out. If you have a high powered blender (like a Vitamix), add a little milk with the cubes, and blend, using the stopper to push the cubes down until smooth. Do not over-blend! Add chocolate chips after blending.

If you do not have a Vitamix, you can make this with a stick blender. Place cubes in a re-sealable plastic bag and seal. Pound the frozen cubes with a hammer or flat side of a meat tenderizer until flattened. Place the flattened cube pieces in a bowl, and use a stick blender to mix, adding milk if needed. Add chocolate chips after blending.

**Variations:
Chocolate ice cream: blend in a few tablespoons of cocoa powder in place of the spinach. Omit the peppermint, or leave it in. Freeze in ice cube trays, and follow the same directions as above.

Vanilla ice cream: Omit spinach, peppermint and chocolate pieces. Blend the milk with 1-2 tsp. vanilla extract. Freeze in ice cube trays, and follow the same directions as above.

No Roll Pie Crust #1

Rolling pie crusts has never been my specialty, even when I ate gluten. When I started eating gluten-free, I found out that rolling gluten-free pie crusts was especially challenging. I started concocting recipes to make it easier for me to have pies without all the work.

1/3 cup rice flour (brown or white)
½ cup tapioca flour
1/3 cup potato starch
1 tsp. xanthan gum
1 Tbsp. sugar or xylitol
1 ½ Tbsp. arrowroot powder or cornstarch
¼ tsp. salt
1/3 cup ghee or casein-free margarine
1 egg, beaten
½ tsp. lemon juice

Preheat oven to 350°. Mix dry ingredients together in a mixing bowl. Cut in the ghee or margarine, and mix until crumbly. Add the egg and lemon juice and mix well. Press dough into a pie plate and poke the crust with a fork.

Bake for 10 minutes, or until the pie crust is lightly browned. Fill with your choice of filling.

<u>Fruit Pie</u>

1 gluten-free single pie crust recipe, or the No Roll Pie Crust #1 or No Roll Pie Crust #2
5 cups fresh or frozen fruit (peaches, blueberries, strawberries, etc.)**
1/3 – 2/3 cup sugar or xylitol (if using low sugar, use 1/3 cup sugar or xylitol and ½ tsp. liquid stevia)
2 Tbsp. arrowroot powder or cornstarch
¼ cup water plus 3 Tbsp., divided (do not add the ¼ cup if using frozen fruit)

If using frozen fruit, thaw the fruit and drain all but 1 cup of the juice. Place the fruit in a pan, along with ¼ cup water if using fresh fruit, or the 1 cup of the juice if using frozen fruit. Cook until bubbly, then add the sugar or xylitol and stevia, if using.

Mix arrowroot or cornstarch with the 3 Tbsp. of water. Add to the fruit mix. Cook and stir until very thick. Pour into a pie shell and chill.

**Note: Certain fruits like strawberries are very watery. If mixture still does not thicken, add 1-2 more Tbsp. of arrowroot or cornstarch to a small amount of water, and add again to pan until mixture thickens.

No Roll Pie Crust #2

1/3 cup almond flour
½ cup tapioca flour
1/3 cup potato starch
1 tsp. xanthan gum
1 Tbsp. arrowroot powder or cornstarch
2 Tbsp. sugar or xylitol
½ tsp. salt
¼ cup olive oil
2-3 Tbsp. dairy-free milk (more if needed)

Preheat oven to 350°. Mix dry ingredients together in a bowl. Add in the olive oil and mix until crumbly. Add the milk and mix well. Press into a pie plate and poke holes in the crust with a fork.

Bake the pie crust for 12-14 minutes, or until the crust is lightly browned. Fill with pie filling of your choice.

No Crust Pumpkin Pie

I have used several different gluten-free flours with this, and all have worked well except for tapioca. With the crunchy, sweet topping, you won't miss the crust!

1 15 ounce can pumpkin
1½ cups dairy-free milk
2 eggs
¼ cup xylitol or coconut sugar
½ tsp. liquid stevia (or ½ cup sugar)
1/3 cup gluten-free flour
½ tsp. baking powder
½ tsp. xanthan gum
1 tsp. cinnamon
½ tsp. nutmeg
1/8 tsp. ground cloves
1/8 tsp. ground ginger
1/8 tsp. salt
2 tsp. vanilla

Topping:
¼ cup coconut sugar or brown sugar
¼ cup chopped walnuts or pecans
1 Tbsp. ghee or casein-free margarine

Preheat oven to 350°. Place pie ingredients (minus toppings) in blender in order listed. Blend until smooth. Pour into greased pie plate. Mix topping ingredients in a small bowl, and sprinkle on top of pie. Bake for 55-60 minutes, or until knife inserted near center comes out clean.

Peach Cobbler

Filling:
2 large cans peaches, drained (reserve ¼ cup liquid)
¼ cup xylitol, sugar or honey
½ tsp. liquid stevia (or replace stevia and above sweetener with ½ cup sugar)
1 ½ Tbsp. arrowroot powder or cornstarch
1 tsp. vanilla

Biscuit topping:
1 cup gluten-free flour blend (p. 32)
¼ cup sugar or xylitol
1 tsp. baking powder
1 tsp. xanthan gum
1 tsp. cinnamon
3 Tbsp. oil
1 egg, beaten
¼ cup dairy-free milk

In a saucepan, add the peaches, xylitol or sugar, stevia (if using), and vanilla. Mix the ¼ cup reserved liquid from the peaches with the 1 ½ Tbsp. arrowroot or cornstarch. Add to the saucepan, and cook until thickened and bubbly. Put filling in a casserole dish or 8 x 8 inch pan.

Mix flour, sugar or xylitol, baking powder, xanthan gum and cinnamon. Add the oil and mix until it resembles coarse crumbs. Combine egg and milk. Add to flour mix and stir until just moistened. Drop onto hot fruit and bake at 350° for 30-35 minutes.

Chocolate Peanut Butter Pie

4 cups dairy-free milk, divided
½ cup honey
½ cup xylitol or sugar
½ cup peanut butter (I used the natural kind)
¼ cup cocoa powder (carob can be substituted for the cocoa)
½ tsp. salt
1 tsp. vanilla
6 Tbsp. arrowroot powder or cornstarch
Pre-baked single piecrust, No Roll Pie Crust #1, or No Roll Pie Crust #2

Place 3½ cups milk in a saucepan, along with honey, xylitol or sugar, peanut butter, cocoa powder, salt and vanilla. Bring to a boil. Mix arrowroot or cornstarch with remaining ½ cup milk. Add to the saucepan, and cook and stir until thickened.

Cool slightly, then pour into the pre-baked pie shell and chill before serving.

Blueberry Coffee Cake

I usually try and cut back on sugar in recipes, but this is one exception where I don't. Compared to a lot of recipes, this one actually isn't as loaded with sugar as most. I made this for my church life group class, and no one could tell that it was gluten-free. My daughter loves it so much that she prefers it for her birthday instead of cake!

2 cups gluten-free flour blend (p. 32)
¾ cup sugar
1 Tbsp. baking powder
½ tsp. salt
1 tsp. xanthan gum
¼ cup coconut oil
¾ cup dairy-free milk
1 egg
2 cups fresh or frozen blueberries

Crumb topping:
½ cup sugar
½ tsp. cinnamon
1/3 cup gluten-free flour blend
¼ cup ghee or casein-free margarine, softened

Glaze:
1 cup powdered sugar
hot water
1 tsp. vanilla

Preheat oven to 350°. Mix flour, sugar, baking powder, salt, xanthan gum, coconut oil, milk and egg with an electric mixer. Beat 30 seconds. Carefully stir in blueberries.
Spread batter into a greased 8 x 11 inch or 9 x 9 inch baking pan. Mix crumb topping ingredients together and sprinkle over batter. Bake for 45-50 minutes, or until toothpick inserted near center comes out clean.

After you remove the coffee cake from the oven, mix glaze ingredients, adding a teaspoon of hot water at a time until the mixture is thin enough to pour. Drizzle over the coffee cake. Serve warm.

Brownies

¾ cup gluten-free flour blend (p. 32)
¼ cup cocoa powder (carob powder can be used in place of cocoa)
½ tsp. baking powder
½ tsp. salt
1 tsp. xanthan gum
2 eggs
½ cup coconut oil
½ cup honey
½ tsp. stevia (or use 1 cup sugar in place of the honey and stevia)
2 tsp. vanilla

Preheat oven to 350°. In a mixing bowl, add flour, cocoa powder, baking powder, salt and xanthan gum. Mix well to combine ingredients. In a separate bowl, with an electric mixer cream the eggs, coconut oil, honey, stevia (if using), and vanilla. If using sugar in place of honey and stevia, mix the sugar in with eggs and oil. Add the egg mixture to the dry mixture, and mix well to combine.

Pour into a greased 8 x 8 inch pan, and bake for 10-15 minutes. You do not want to cook these long if you want them a little gooey. Do not overcook them, or they will be dry.

Strawberry Puff

Fruit mix:
32 ounces frozen strawberries, thawed (do not drain)
½ cup xylitol
¼ tsp. stevia (or 1 cup sugar in place of xylitol and stevia)
1 tsp. vanilla

Biscuit topping:
2 cups gluten-free flour blend (p. 32)
2 Tbsp. xylitol or sugar
1 Tbsp. baking powder
1 tsp. xanthan gum
½ tsp. salt
1/3 cup olive oil
2/3 cup dairy-free milk (use more if needed)

Sugar topping:
2 Tbsp. xylitol or sugar
1 tsp. cinnamon

Preheat oven to 350°. For fruit mix, in a bowl, combine strawberries (along with the juice), xylitol, stevia (or 1 cup sugar, if using in place of the xylitol and stevia) and vanilla. Pour the fruit mix into an ungreased 9 x 13 inch baking pan.
For biscuit topping, mix flour, xylitol or sugar, baking powder, xanthan gum and salt in a bowl. Mix the olive oil and milk in a separate bowl, and pour into flour mixture. Stir until just moistened. Drop dough by spoonfuls onto fruit.
Mix the sugar topping ingredients together and sprinkle over the dough. Bake for 35-40 minutes, or until toothpick inserted in topping comes out clean.

Custard Pie

Pre-baked single piecrust, No Roll Pie Crust #1, or No Roll Pie Crust #2
4 eggs
½ cup honey
½ tsp. stevia (or ½ cup sugar in place of the stevia)
1 tsp. vanilla
1/8 tsp. salt
2 cups dairy-free milk
Nutmeg

Preheat oven to 350°. In a bowl, beat eggs slightly. Stir in honey, stevia (or sugar) vanilla and salt. Gradually stir in milk. Mix well.

Pour the filling into the pre-baked pie shell, and sprinkle with nutmeg. Bake for 1 hour. As the custard bakes, it will puff up high as it cooks, so don't be alarmed if this happens. It will settle to normal after cooking.

Chill the pie after it cools.

Fruit Crisp

Fruit mix:
5 cups sliced, peeled apples, pears or peaches, frozen peach slices, or fresh or frozen blueberries (if frozen, thaw, but do not drain)
4 Tbsp. xylitol or sugar

Topping mix:
½ cup gluten-free flour (whichever kind you prefer)
¼ cup xylitol or sugar
¼ cup coconut sugar or brown sugar
½ tsp. cinnamon
¼ tsp. nutmeg
¼ cup ghee, casein-free margarine, or coconut oil
½ cup walnuts of pecans, chopped fine

Preheat oven to 375°. For filling, thaw fruit if frozen, but do not drain. Place fruit in a round casserole dish. Stir in the 4 Tbsp. xylitol or sugar.

For topping, combine flour, xylitol or sugar, coconut sugar or brown sugar, cinnamon, and nutmeg. Cut in ghee, margarine or coconut oil with a fork or pastry blender until the mixture is crumbly. Stir in chopped nuts and mix well. Sprinkle on the top of the fruit.

Bake for 40-45 minutes, or until the fruit is tender and the topping is browned.

Baked Apples

The original recipe for this was loaded with sugar and butter. I modified it to be lower in sugar, and dairy-free.

4 large baking apples (such as Jonathan, Cortland, Golden Delicious, or Gala)
¼ cup coconut sugar or brown sugar
1 tsp. cinnamon
¼ cup raisins
¼ cup chopped pecans or walnuts
3/4 cup apple juice, brought to a boil
1 Tbsp. ghee or casein-free margarine

Preheat oven to 350°. Wash the apples and remove the cores, but do not cut all the way through. Leave about ¼ to ½ inch of the core in the bottom of the apples. In a small bowl, combine the sugar, cinnamon, raisins and nuts.

Place the apples in an 8 x 8 inch baking dish, and stuff each apple with the sugar mixture. Top each with a dot of the ghee or margarine. Add the hot apple juice to the pan. Bake for 15 minutes. Baste the apples with the apple juice. Bake the apples for another 15-20 minutes, or until the apples are tender but not mushy. Baste the apples with the juice from the pan before serving.

Rice Krispie Treats

Our family loves Rice Krispie Treats, but they are loaded with sugar. This is a healthy alternative.

2/3 cup peanut butter or any nut butter
2/3 cup honey
6 cups GFCFSF crispy rice cereal (Nature's Path or Barbara's Bakery)
1 tsp. vanilla extract

Combine the peanut butter, honey and vanilla in a saucepan. Heat over low heat, stirring until mixture melts. Watch carefully so that it doesn't burn. Pour the mixture over the cereal and mix well. Make sure that the cereal is evenly coated.

Press the mixture into a 13 x 9 x 2 inch baking dish that has been sprayed with nonstick spray. Allow to cool before cutting.

These will need to keep in the fridge so that they don't get too soft.

Applesauce Cake

2¼ cup gluten-free flour blend (p. 32)
1 tsp. salt
1 tsp. baking soda
1 tsp. cinnamon
½ tsp. xanthan gum
½ cup olive oil
1 cup molasses
1 egg
1 cup applesauce

Preheat oven to 350°. Combine flour, salt, baking soda, cinnamon, and xanthan gum in a mixing bowl. Add the oil, molasses, egg and applesauce. Mix well.

Bake in a greased 8 x 8 inch square pan for 35-45 minutes, or until toothpick inserted near center comes out clean.

Kopykat Kit Kat bars

It is hard to imagine that these are actually healthy! This recipe makes a large amount.

Wafer:
4 egg whites (room temperature)
1 ½ tsp. vanilla
¼ tsp. xanthan gum
½ tsp. liquid stevia (replace with 1 cup sugar if you do not like stevia)
3 T. honey

Place egg whites, vanilla and xanthan gum in a mixing bowl*. Start beating and drizzle in stevia and honey. If you are adding sugar in place of stevia, add it slowly, a little bit at a time. Beat for 10 minutes or until stiff peaks form. Place mixture in a re-sealable plastic bag and snip a corner with scissors. Squeeze out long rectangle shapes onto parchment paper-lined baking sheets. Bake at 300° for 40 minutes. Watch carefully so that they do not burn. If they start getting too brown, drop temperature down to 275°. After 40 minutes, turn heat down to 200° for another 30 minutes. Turn off heat and open the oven door. Allow to cool with the oven door open for 1 hour. **Humidity can affect the crispiness of these bars. If it is very humid, it may be harder to keep them crisp.

Chocolate coating:
4 oz. unsweetened bakers chocolate (I used Sunspire baking chocolate)
½ tsp. liquid stevia (replace with ½ cup sugar if you do not like stevia)
¼ cup honey
¼ cup coconut oil

Melt coating ingredients over low heat, stirring constantly until melted. Allow to cool slightly. Dip wafers in the coating, and place back on the parchment paper. Place in the refrigerator until hardened. Store bars in the refrigerator.

*I used a stand mixer for this recipe. I found a Sunbeam stand mixer at amazon.com for under $40.00. For recipes like this, it makes it so much less time consuming.

Chocolate Bars

These are both healthy and tasty, and very versatile. I break the bars up and use them like chocolate chips that can be used in cookies, or ice cream. They can also be melted and used for chocolate sauce or syrup.

1/2 cup cocoa powder
1 cup coconut oil, heated just until melted
Honey and stevia to taste
Chopped nuts (optional)

Mix cocoa, coconut oil and honey and stevia until there are no lumps. Gently stir in chopped nuts and peppermint oil if using. Pour into a parchment lined 8 x 8 inch pan. Put in the freezer to harden. These need to be kept in the fridge or freezer, or they will be too soft.

*Variations:
-Add 1 drop of peppermint oil for mint chocolate
-Use ¼ cup carob powder in place of cocoa powder
-Use ½ cup mesquite flour in place, or ¼ cup mesquite flour and ¼ cup cocoa powder for a caramel flavored bar

Pumpkin Custard

1 15 ounce can pumpkin
1 cup dairy-free milk
4 eggs
1/4 tsp. nutmeg
1 tsp. cinnamon
1/2 tsp. liquid stevia (or ½ cup sugar if you do not like stevia)
1/2 tsp. vanilla
¼ cup honey

Preheat oven to 325°. Grease either small custard cups or a casserole type dish. In a double boiler, add all ingredients and whisk well to mix. Heat the mixture to 150° (use a candy thermometer). Pour into the small custard cups or in the casserole dish. Put the cups or the dish in a larger pan, and fill the pan 1 inch full of hot water. Be careful not to spill any water into the custard. Bake for 55-60 minutes, or until the custard tests done.

Chocolate Balls

Almond butter
Coconut oil, heated to just melted
Cocoa or carob powder
Honey or xylitol
Stevia
Shredded coconut (optional)

Mix desired amounts together. Taste to see if it is sweet enough, and thick enough to form into balls. Scoop into balls and put in fridge.

Apple Streusel Pie

1 premade pie crust (one of the no-roll ones works well)
5 large apples
1 tsp. lemon juice
1 tsp. vanilla extract
5 packets stevia (I used the NOW brand...if you don't like stevia, replace with ½ cup sugar)
1/4 c. coconut sugar (or xylitol or regular sugar)
1 Tbsp. arrowroot powder or cornstarch
1/2 Tbsp. cinnamon

Streusel Topping:
3/4 c. gluten-free flour blend (p. 32)
1/3 c. coconut sugar (or xylitol or regular sugar)
2 packets stevia (replace with ¼ cup sugar if you don't like stevia)
1/4 t. cinnamon
1/2 c. coconut oil
2/3 c. chopped walnuts

Peel and slice apples, and place in a large bowl. Add lemon juice and vanilla to the apples and carefully stir. Sprinkle the stevia, coconut sugar, arrowroot and cinnamon over apples and stir carefully until evenly coated. Pour apple mixture into the prepared pie crust. Mix the streusel topping until crumbly, then sprinkle over the top of the apple mixture. Bake at 350 degrees for 55-60 minutes.

Chocolate No Bake Bars

These are a healthy version of the sugar and dairy laden cookies I used to eat all the time as a child. I tried these out on the kids in our neighborhood, and they came back for seconds!

1/4 cup cocoa
1/8 tsp. pure stevia powder or ½ tsp. NOW stevia glycerite liquid
3/4 cup honey (replace with 2 cups of sugar if you do not like honey or stevia)
1/2 cup coconut oil
3/4 cup nondairy milk
1/2 cup peanut butter
1 tsp. vanilla
3 cups gluten-free rolled oats

Place all ingredients minus the vanilla and oats in a large saucepan. Melt and stir the ingredients over medium/high heat until melted and bubbly. Take off the heat and add the vanilla and oats. Spread into a greased 8 x 8 pan. Refrigerate until hardened.

Cut into squares. Keep refrigerated.

Carrot Cake

1/3 c. coconut oil
1/4 c. honey
3/4 c. applesauce
3/4 tsp. liquid stevia (I used the NOW stevia glycerite)
2 eggs
2/3 c. almond flour
1/3 c. coconut flour
1/2 tsp. baking powder
1/2 tsp. baking soda
1/4 tsp. salt
1 tsp. cinnamon
1 c. finely chopped or grated carrots

Frosting:
1 cup raw cashews, soaked in water for at least 6 hours
¼ cup water
½ to 1 tsp. vanilla extract
Stevia and honey to taste

In a mixing bowl, cream together coconut oil, honey, applesauce, stevia and eggs. Mix dry ingredients in a separate bowl, then add to the creamed mixture. Fold in carrots. Press into an 8 x 8 greased baking pan. Bake at 350 degrees for 30 minutes, or until tests done. Allow to cool.

For frosting, drain cashews. Place cashews in a blender along with the ¼ cup of water. Blend well until creamy, scraping the sides of the blender with a spatula when necessary. Add vanilla, and sweetener, sweetening to taste and blend again. Frost cooled cake. Refrigerate if you are not going to serve it right away.

Chocolate Chip Cookies

1 c. shortening (I used Spectrum Naturals, which is non-hydrogenated palm oil)
1/2 cup xylitol
1/2 cup packed coconut sugar
1/8 tsp. stevia
1 tsp. vanilla
2 eggs
1 1/2 cup gluten free flour blend (p. 32)
3/4 cup almond flour
1 1/2 tsp. xanthan gum
1 tsp. salt
1 tsp. baking powder
1 tsp. baking soda
1/2-1 cup chocolate chips (I used a dark chocolate very low sugar bar and broke it into pieces)

Cream the shortening, xylitol, coconut sugar, stevia, and vanilla. Add eggs and blend well. Mix the dry ingredients together in a bowl, and slowly add to the creamed ingredients. Fold in chocolate chips/pieces.

Drop dough onto ungreased cookie sheets by spoonfuls, flattening the dough a bit with the back of the spoon. Bake at 350 degrees for 12 minutes, or until golden brown. Remove immediately from the cookie sheet to cool on wire racks.

Note: Because of the almond flour in this recipe, I store the cookies in the fridge. This recipe made 2 dozen cookies when I made them.

Candy Cane Kisses

These are very addictive. They are crispy, not chewy, and are hard to describe what they compare to. They are like small, melt-in-your-mouth crispy cookies. These are sensitive to humidity, and may turn out softer if you are in a hot and humid environment.

4 egg whites, room temperature
1/4 tsp. salt
1/4 tsp. cream of tartar
1/4 cup honey
1/2 tsp. liquid stevia (I used NOW stevia glycerite)
1 tsp. vanilla extract
1 or 2 peppermint crushed candy canes, or a small handful of peppermint candies, crushed

In a mixing bowl, beat egg whites until foamy. Add the salt and cream of tartar, and while beating, slowly drizzle in the honey, stevia and vanilla. Beat until stiff and glossy (about 10 minutes). Spoon the meringue mix into a re-sealable plastic bag (you can also use a pastry bag). Cut a small hole in the corner of the re-sealable bag. Squeeze small kisses (I did about 1 1/2 inch sizes) onto parchment or Silpat lined baking sheets. Sprinkle the kisses with the crushed candy canes or peppermints. Bake at 225 degrees for 1 1/2 hours. If they start getting too browned, turn the heat down farther. They will still be soft after cooking. Turn oven off, and allow the kisses to cool in the oven for at least an hour. After cooled and hardened, remove them from the baking sheets and store in an airtight container.

Special Thanks and Acknowledgements:

Cover pictures by Joyce McGuire and Jennifer Wood

Cover design by Jason Brown of JsBrown Studio

I wanted to thank my wonderful husband and daughter for being my best cheerleaders (and taste testers!). You are both such a blessing to me, and I am so thankful for you. I could never have done this without the support you gave me. I love you both so much! Thank you also to my mother-in-law for trying out so many of the recipes for me, and my father-in-law for taste-testing them, for my sister who listened to me brainstorm for hours, and for my parents for their support through this, and for coming over and taste-testing my cooking. I love you! I am so blessed to have you all in my life! I want to thank my Lord and Savior Jesus Christ, who gave His life for us on the cross so that we might have eternal life. Thank you, Lord for giving me the ability to come up with the recipes in the first place. I could not have done it without your help.

Romans 10:9

About the Author:

Jennifer Wood lives in the Midwest with her family. When she isn't in her kitchen working hard on new recipe creations, she is homeschooling, gardening, or enjoying the outdoors.

CPSIA information can be obtained
at www.ICGtesting.com
Printed in the USA
LVHW060910021218
598965LV00014B/756/P